PRAISE FOR ROBERT SANDFORD'S
WATER, WEATHER AND THE MOUNTAIN WEST

Every politician in western Canada should be locked in a room until he or she has read this book. Bob Sandford has followed the water from the headwaters to the drain pipe, from the heavens and into the hell of wasteful, arrogant neglect. Seeing our Canadian myths about limitless lakes of pristine water darted like so many helium-filled balloons is harrowing, but Sandford follows up with a long list of thoughtful solutions that all of us need to consider; our survival and prosperity, as well as the survival of the entire ecosystem, is at stake. And let's all stop drinking bottled water as a first step; read and find out why.

> — Sid Marty, author of *Switchbacks: True Stories from the Canadian Rockies, Men for the Mountains* and *Leaning on the Wind: Under the Spell of the Great Chinook*

Bob Sandford's eloquently written book will shock those who believe we have water to spare. It should be required reading for Canadians, especially politicians who continue to dither about controlling climate change.

> — Dr. David Schindler,
> Killam Memorial Professor of Ecology,
> University of Alberta

Myths of abundant and stationary water supplies have influenced water use and management in the Canadian West. These perceptions are part misconception and part physical reality. Since European settlement, western Canadians have enjoyed surplus water from retreating glaciers and an absence of prolonged drought relative to other centuries. But that is about to change, with stunning potential consequences for the West. This book tells why.

> — Dr. David Sauchyn,
> Prairie Adaptation Research Collaborative,
> University of Regina

Water,
Weather
and the
Mountain West

Robert William Sandford

Rocky
Mountain Books
VANCOUVER · VICTORIA · CALGARY

Rocky Mountain Books
#108 – 17665 66A Avenue
Surrey, BC V3S 2A7
www.rmbooks.com

Rocky Mountain Books
PO Box 468
Custer, WA
98240-0468

Library and Archives Canada Cataloguing in Publication

Sandford, Robert W.
    Water, weather and the Mountain West / Robert William Sandford.

Includes bibliographical references.
ISBN 978-1-894765-93-0

    1. Water-supply--Canada, Western. 2. Water conservation--Canada, Western.
3. Water table--Climatic factors--Canada, Western. I. Title.

GF511.S26 2007   433.91'009712   C2007-902921-3

Library of Congress Control Number: 2007932008

Text edited, designed and typeset by Joe Wilderson
Cover design by Jacqui Thomas
Cover photos by Slawomir Jastrzebski ("Drop of Water")
    and Ashok Rodrigues ("Turquoise Mountain Pools") / iStockphoto

Printed in Canada

Rocky Mountain Books acknowledges the financial support for its publishing program from the Government of Canada through the Book Publishing Industry Development Program (BPIDP), Canada Council for the Arts, and the province of British Columbia through the British Columbia Arts Council and the Book Publishing Tax Credit.

Canada Council
for the Arts

Conseil des Arts
du Canada

BRITISH
COLUMBIA
ARTS COUNCIL

This book has been produced on 100% post-consumer recycled paper, processed chlorine free and printed with vegetable-based dyes.

≈

Contents

*For Reid,
Amery and Landon,
who will inherit the mountains
and the water, but a different climate*

Invocation

≈

Through Mist and Rainbow the Water Speaks

NEITHER OF THEM HAD EVER SEEN SUCH A THING. It was as if an entire river had somehow been turned on end. Right before their very eyes, a pillar of water half a kilometre tall crashed so hard into the earth that the ground shook. The continuous thunder was so loud it made their chests vibrate. It was as if the roar had taken up residence within them and their hearts were singing the song of the falling water. Above this river tumbling out of the sky was a mountain so tall it made them dizzy to look that far straight up. What seemed impossible from their vantage was that the water fell continuously, without apparent beginning and seemingly without end. It was like being beneath a colossal fully opened tap.

Haloed in rainbows and drenched in fine mist the two stood together against the roar, shaking their heads slowly in time with their awe. They had been told that this river falling out of the sky had an Aboriginal name and that the name was an expression of utter wonderment. Takakkaw, it was called: "it is magnificent." Indeed it was.

One of the two was from Jordan and was in Canada to plead for help in saving his country's namesake river before an international forum of water experts. Before them he argued quietly that the Jordan River — barely a car's length wide and the lifeblood of his entire country — is dying. This calm and competent man stood with grave dignity before this forum to say that, without international help, the Jordan River will be gone in a decade and the whole fragile political framework of the Middle East could collapse into its dry bed. His speech was followed by a silence so complete you could hear birds singing outside. Who could comprehend such loss?

The other man was from sub-Saharan Africa, where 50,000 people die every year from want of water or from the diseases borne by the small but contaminated amounts available to them. He was in Canada to remind the rest of the world of the global water crisis and what it meant to those two billion souls on this planet who either don't have reliable access to water or who are forced by circumstances to drink water dangerous to their health.

The two returned from the falls soaked and giddy as though they had somehow found their way into the centre of one of the great forces of nature and come back to tell the tale. We couldn't get the grins off their faces. The glow lasted all the way back to Banff. What happened could only be described as one more epic, life-changing adventure in what locals call "Great Days in the Rockies." But something haunted us all.

Even though it was mid-September, Takakkaw Falls was in full splendour. Full splendour in this context means it was in full spate. It was as big on this day as it would have been in the peak of snowmelt in June. In other words, the Daly Glacier, which feeds the falls after the winter snow has melted, was, even in September, melting away at a rate matched only by the hottest summer day. None of the water experts standing at the base of the falls had to be told why this was happening. Our climate is changing and the first and boldest evidence of this has become obvious at the poles and in the high places of our mountains. What we were seeing at Takakkaw Falls was a direct effect of global warming.

The falls we visited in the Yoho Valley were stunning. This was not just because the volume of the water and the sheer spectacle of the setting were such that it slowed the mind simply beholding it. What was happening was also symbolic. That such melt was occurring so late in the season symbolized the end of the climate regime as we have known it for hundreds of years. It was as if we had put our finger on the pulse of the world and discovered its heart rate was three times normal. It was as if we had taken the Earth's temperature and discovered it had a fever.

Though it was spectacular to see the falls in full flood and to feel the power of the falling water, seeing it in such monumental display in mid-September was deeply troubling. The display of rapid melt at Takakkaw Falls only amplified the significance of what we had seen elsewhere. Throughout the mountain West we are losing water we had in the bank at a rate that is almost impossible to comprehend. It is as if the tap really has been left full open and the wealth of the West is draining away as fast as the rivers can accommodate its loss. We are on the way to a warmer West and — climate-change models notwithstanding — it is likely going to be a drier and drier region as temperatures rise. And drier — for the uninitiated — means less water.

One cannot stand below such falls in full knowledge of what we have done to the world without becoming circumspect. What we saw before us on this September day was deceiving. These waters are not the great thundering expression of pristine nature that we might have liked to think. We are the ones causing the ice to melt. We are causing Takakkaw to fall when it shouldn't be falling. It is we who turned September into summer. It is we who turned on the tap and let it run. But this water does not fall continuously, nor does it exist without end. By turning up the heat we have altered the Western water cycle. It is we who may run out of water as a consequence. We are joined together — all of us — by weather and water. No matter where you live in this great lone land, weather *is* water.

Dropping out of the sky from less blessed places, visitors from abroad instantly see what we sometimes forget. What makes Canada utterly unique in the world's imagination is that water exists plentifully here, in all its remarkable forms. Without abundant water, we would be a very different nation and a very different people. In the world's imagination, ours is a land of ice and snow, lakes, wild rivers, glaciers and icefields. That doesn't have to change, but we do.

Water in the Canadian West is telling us something. Our culture has been carried downstream from its source. Where once we carried around inside our minds a map of the country as defined by watersheds, we no longer think of ourselves as an empire of rivers. Most Canadians still believe the myth of limitless abundance. Many of us take water completely for granted. Too many of us turn on the tap now without thinking. We forget that our identity as a people is defined by what water is and by what it does.

If the myth of limitless abundance of Canadian resources is to be dispelled, that process will likely begin in Canada's western mountains. On the eastern slopes of the Rockies and on the dry interior plains, we are approaching the limits of water availability and are now beginning to understand how important mountain water is to us and to the rest of the West.

Our water is telling us that some of the most cherished images we hold of ourselves are about to be challenged. In re-evaluating what water means to us, it may well be that we will be forced to re-evaluate the Canadian style of life. To fully understand emerging problems associated with water quality and availability in Canada, we have to return to our cultural headwaters to rethink what water means to us. Properly viewed, this could be a very positive development.

In returning to our cultural headwaters, we can reaffirm our relationship to place and grow closer to the landscapes and water-courses that were the founding inspiration of our uniqueness as a people. In so doing, we can compare the West we had in the past with the West we have now so that we can decide upon the kind of West we want to create for our children and their children.

One: Water, Weather and the West

Dispelling the Myth of Limitless Abundance

THE WORLD FACES A LOT OF PROBLEMS TODAY and many of them relate to water. When the United Nations established its Millennium goals, improving the global water supply was an important priority. Presently there are a billion people on Earth who do not have reliable access to fresh water. There are two billion who do not have adequate sanitation.

The global community has been trying to address these challenges for a very long time. In response to growing problems associated with water supply and quality worldwide, the UN declared 2003 the International Year of Fresh Water. In 2005 the UN Decade of Action Water for Life was declared, as a means of responding to what has now been identified as a full-blown global water crisis. Some 85 countries are engaged in this initiative.

The purpose of the UN Water for Life partnership in Canada is to put Canadian water issues in a global context. The goal of this initiative, which includes dozens of government and private sector partners, is to learn from others so that issues of water availability and quality don't limit our social and economic development in Canada in the future. While this will be surprising to many, preventing water scarcity from limiting our future may not be as easy as it sounds, particularly in the Canadian West.

As the Chair of the UN Water for Life Decade of Action initiative in Canada, it has been my pleasure to travel from the Queen Charlotte Islands in British Columbia to the east coast of Newfoundland examining first-hand how we manage water in Canada. The first and only question I am asked no matter where I go is whether or not it is even possible to have a water problem in Canada. "We have a quarter of the world's fresh water," journalists declare; "how can we possibly have a problem with water?"

My answer is this: yes, it is true that in comparison to the rest of the world, Canada has adequate water, and so does the United States. But it is not limitless as we so often want to believe. We have about 2,850 cubic kilometres, or roughly 6.5 per cent of the world's total *renewable* fresh water resource. By renewable I mean water that is replaced in any given year through rain and snow-fall. The rest of our water is stored in lakes or in ice or permanent snow. It is fossil water, so to speak, in that it is left over from an earlier, wetter geological age. This is water in the bank. Once we spend this water, it is gone.

Even a small increase in temperature could cause the loss of this stored water. With higher temperatures glaciers will disappear and standing fossil water in northern lakes will evaporate. As this happens — as it is bound to — the hydrology of the entire country will change.

The Canadian myth of limitless abundance of clean, fresh water is also belied by its distribution. Most of our freshwater resources are not located where most of us live. About 65 per cent of Canada's water is in the north of the country, while 90 per cent of the population lives within 300 kilometres of the u.s. border.

Many Canadians find it astounding to discover that the regions where most Canadians live are not water abundant. In fact, excluding the Alaskan contribution to u.s. water supply, the 48 contiguous u.s. states receive 57 per cent of the national supply, about 1½ times more water per capita than is available to the Canadian population living in the southern part of Canada.

What this suggests is that, in southern Canada, we don't have as much water as we may have thought. If the Americans want our water, they will have to go to the same place we will have to go if we want more: the Canadian north. And that will be very costly, as diverting water from northern rivers will, in many regions, require pumping the water uphill.

For these reasons, it is important that we dispel the myth of limitless abundance of water in this country. If we don't, we will make policy decisions based on false assumptions of abundance that could have huge ecological, economic and political consequences.

There is another myth we need to dispel, and that is that we live in a land of natural, clean water. Growing populations and economies are putting pressure on both the quality and the availability of water in many parts of Canada. In addition to not always being where we want it when we want it, our water is not always as clean as we might like to think.

In relative terms, Canada is not keeping up with emerging drinking-water quality issues. In fact, we trust our own myths of limitless abundance and high quality to such an extent that we often have trouble seeing what is happening right in front of our very eyes. Outsiders are often more objective observers of how successfully we are managing our much-vaunted fresh water resources.

Fred Pearce is a well-respected water expert from Britain who wrote a book in 2006 called *When Rivers Run Dry: Journeys into the Heart of the World's Water Crisis.* The Canadian edition of his book begins with an assessment of the water situation in Canada. His conclusions are startling:

> No country on Earth has such contrasts of drought and water plenty as Canada. None has so much water ready and available for use. But Canada is learning that national statistics do not begin to portray the complexity of its relationship with its most vital resource.
>
> On the Mackenzie and the Rupert and the South Saskatchewan, in the leaking water mains of Montreal and the emptying reservoirs of Vancouver, down Canada's turbines and toilets, a new reality is emerging.
>
> It is a reality in which water is in increasingly short supply in some places at some times, where water suddenly has a real value rather than being an unlimited resource — and where rivers truly can run dry.

Is there a water crisis in Canada? No, not compared to other places. But in parts of Canada, especially in the water-scarce West, we have all the elements to create one. The reason we do not yet have a water crisis is that there is still a lot of slack we can take up in our systems to prevent crisis. We can take up this slack through water conservation and management strategies that will ensure that water issues do not limit our social and economic future. Because we have taken water for granted and waste so much of it, we still have a little room to move. But once we have accomplished as much as we can through conservation, we will be facing water scarcity, just like many other parts of the world. Then things will get interesting.

Are we preparing for these eventualities? Are we taking up the slack in our systems? Are we doing enough to prevent a water crisis in the Canadian West? The answers to these questions depend upon where you live and your perspective on what you have and what you want. If I were to characterize the general Canadian situation, it might be in the following way.

Ask most politicians if water issues in their jurisdiction are under control and they will inevitably say, "No problem, everything has been taken care of. It's all good." In response to this same question, senior government bureaucrats will often say, "Well, not quite." Some senior water managers will say, "Actually, not at all." Some scientists will say, "Look out, we're headed for a wreck." Local watershed groups will invariably say there are problems; that's why such groups exist. Farmers and big industrial users will say, "Don't worry, we've figured out how to solve the problems — at least for ourselves."

What is interesting about this is that at any given moment in any given watershed, all of these perspectives may well be valid. Seen from the perspective of a single jurisdiction, things appear to be working, for the moment at least. But the writing is on the wall. The way we have atomized responsibility for managing water does not allow for any one body to fully comprehend what is actually happening to our water resources in terms of the cumulative effects of population growth, landscape change and global warming. Even provincial governments, which in Canada are the ones responsible for water management, have not been able to keep up with the problems we have begun to create for ourselves in the West. Trapped within our own legislative, physical and operational infrastructure, the West may not be able to respond to a water crisis until it is upon us. But water is one thing, weather quite another. Bringing government, industry and the public together on climate change in the Canadian West will be like herding poisonous snakes (watch out for the sharp ends!).

Others Have Been Where We Are Now

THE PROVINCE OF ALBERTA HAS RUN OUT OF WATER in its southern rivers. Every river in Alberta from the Montana border to the Red Deer is fully, if not over-, allocated. For this reason, the government of Alberta is no longer granting new water licences in the South Saskatchewan River Basin.

This means that the only way social and economic development can continue at current rates is if Albertans can take up the slack in the system and do more with the water they have. In other words, provincial prosperity will depend not only on petroleum resources but on how well Albertans learn to manage water.

Though it still remains incomprehensible to many, the moratorium on licensing makes it obvious that if you live in the South Saskatchewan River Basin, water conservation is coming soon to a theatre near you. This suggests also that if you live on the South Saskatchewan downstream from Alberta — that is to say in Saskatchewan or Manitoba — the same conservation measures will also become obligatory in the near future.

This should hardly come as a surprise. Our Western population is growing, we are rapidly altering our landscapes, and our climate is changing. What we are facing here now is not new. It has happened to others elsewhere before.

What is happening in the rest of the world tips us off to the fact that managing water effectively may be more important as an indicator of stability and sustainability than we have imagined in the Canadian West. We have always known we in North America are privileged to have such abundant natural resources. One look at what's happening on the global level makes it even more apparent how fortunate we are to possess so much natural capital.

In terms of the global water situation, it is hard not to be stunned into near silence by what we are seeing happen right in front of our very eyes. What we are facing is, in fact, a world water crisis. On a global scale, soil erosion is exceeding new soil formation by 10 to 40 times. On a planetary scale, we are cutting forests faster than they can grow back. We are also releasing CO_2 faster than nature can absorb it. By 2000, we were exceeding the Earth's regenerative capacity by perhaps 20 per cent.

It is not just traditional environmentalists who are uneasy about this. Economists and policy-makers all over the world are concerned that our excessive demands are consuming the Earth's assets and that in so doing we are, in effect, creating a bubble economy. And a big part of this bubble relates to fresh water or, perhaps more accurately, to food and water.

To meet the food demands that are projected to exist in the world in 2025, it has been estimated that we will need to put an additional 2,000 cubic kilometres of water into irrigation.

This amount is roughly equivalent to 20 times the average annual flow of the Nile. Given current water-use patterns, the total human population that is projected to exist in 2050 will require an estimated 3,800 cubic kilometres of water a year, which is close to all of the fresh water that presently can be withdrawn on Earth. This would mean that the world would lose most of the important environmental services that aquatic ecosystems presently provide on our behalf. Clearly, that is just not going to happen. There is no way we can use all the surface water the planet has to offer. Something will give before we reach that point.

What is really happening here is that human economic and population growth is coming up hard against the limits of water availability. As we would expect in a globally integrated economy, this situation could have significant consequences. One of the great fears being put forward by the United Nations is that environmental degradation will burst the bubble economy and that job and opportunity losses will rise sharply in many places in the world simultaneously, causing spill-over impacts even in those places where environmental decline is not presently an economic issue.

We live very well on this continent, but it is increasingly clear — especially in the Canadian West — that we cannot be insulated from these developments forever. Even if we could miraculously avoid what is happening elsewhere, global problems are going to affect us in ways that will make heavy new demands on how we live.

The implications for the mountain West will ultimately be manifold. They will include impacts that are already beginning to affect a number of important aspects of our way of life. What is happening both globally and regionally to our water supplies has already begun to influence water storage and hydro power generation in the mountain West. These effects are already being felt downstream by agriculture and industry. These impacts are already beginning to affect human settlement patterns, real-estate values, community development and local sense of place. In time this will dramatically affect recreation, tourism and local identity. Changes in hydrological regimes will begin as resource issues. They will then become economic impacts which will affect our social fabric and our political institutions.

We will not be immune to what is happening elsewhere in the world. What is happening to hydrological regimes in other places will also happen here. The first problem we face is that there are more of us, even in Canada, and we are using more and more water. We are altering land-use patterns so quickly in many areas that it is getting harder and more expensive to keep our water clean. An additional threat — and the real wild card — is climate change.

While much is made of the potential of climate change to alter our world, climate is only one factor driving current planetary change. Global warming impacts are likely to be most significant in places where they function as added stresses on natural systems already under heavy pressure from human activities or where landscapes and ecosystems have been degraded, fragmented or compromised in the past. In order to create the West we want, we will have to learn from others who have already been where we are now. We will also want to learn from those who are successfully addressing problems we have not faced before, such as those that will present themselves as climate change alters how much water we have and when it is available to us.

≈

Food and Water

A SIGNIFICANT COMPONENT of our global bubble economy relates to food security. Food production in many places in the world is artificially inflated by unsustainable use of groundwater. Falling water tables and rising temperatures are converging to make it more difficult to expand food production fast enough to keep up with global population growth.

The question the UN is asking globally is this: can the world's farmers bounce back and expand production fast enough to feed 70 million more people each year? Looking at the challenges and their implications, it is going to be difficult.

Farmers today may face temperatures higher than have confronted any generation since agriculture began in the Middle East some 11,000 years ago. Beyond a certain point, increased temperature slows development of many crops. One U.S. study estimated that a 1°C mean annual rise will lower contemporary wheat, rice and corn yields by 10 per cent. Increased temperature also affects water availability. Recent estimates suggest that climate change will increase global water scarcity by 20 per cent.

In addition to high mean temperatures, today's farmers are also the first generation to face widespread aquifer depletion and the resulting loss of irrigation water. The problem of falling water tables is even more difficult than rising temperatures. As world water demand has climbed, water tables in important food-producing countries such as India, China and even the United States have dropped, in some cases dramatically. These countries produce half of the world's grain.

In addition to falling exponentially, water tables are also falling *simultaneously* in many countries. This means shortfalls in grain harvests will occur in many countries at more or less the same time. And they will occur at a time in history when the world's population is growing at a rate equivalent to two Canadas every year.

So what does that mean to us in the West? As countries around the world become water scarce, it will become more and more necessary to import water, not in its raw liquid state, but as water embodied in food. Global experts have predicted that Western Canadian agriculture will have a new and very prominent niche in the global economy — provided it can keep up with solutions to its own water availability and quality challenges related to agricultural practices.

Some experts have predicted that this niche will ultimately be more important to the Western Canadian economy than oil and gas. Whether this will happen is unclear, but what is clear is that it will make it more difficult to assume we can simply take water away from agriculture and use it for other purposes.

While our agricultural promise may be very great, there is no doubt that we have our own worries. Our landscapes are already changing. If the climate continues to warm, landscapes will change even more. Expect some areas in Canada to become semi-arid and other areas to become deserts.

Models of the future climate of the Canadian prairies developed by Dr. David Sauchyn and his colleagues at the Prairie Adaptation Research Collaborative at the University of Regina illustrate how temperature increases will lead to desertification of a sizable area of the Canadian prairies over the coming century. If this projection comes true, the Canadian prairies are going to be a different place than they are today.

The climate models created by Dr. Sauchyn and his colleagues also indicate, however, that there will also be benefits connected with climate change in this region. The average growing season will lengthen. Warmer temperatures are expected to increase the number of heat days, which crops need to mature. The agricultural region on the Great Plains will expand northward into what is now parkland.

There is no question that a longer growing season could be a boon to agriculture. Undoubtedly the production of two crops a year will become a viable option in some years, especially in irrigated areas of the Great Plains and in central British Columbia. Some models go so far as to predict that Canada and Russia may in fact be big winners in terms of agriculture, provided global warming stays within a limited range. Once warming extends beyond 2°C or 3°C, all bets may be off. The most important thing to note, however, is that all future development in agriculture is predicated entirely on how well the industry manages water availability challenges and resolves issues related to water contamination associated with current agricultural practices.

The future success of agriculture is also predicated upon how well we understand both the impacts and the consequences of climate change in the Western Canadian context.

General public reaction to climate change in Canada has been interesting to observe in that it puts human behaviour into relief in fascinating ways. One reaction to climate change, particularly in Alberta, is to simply keep your head down. If you don't notice it and don't talk about it, then it can't be real.

When confronted with an ever-growing mass of facts and our own first-hand observations, many North Americans, for some reason, simply maintain global warming isn't happening. This is interesting in that it is different from how the issue is perceived elsewhere in the world.

Nearly a decade after the Kyoto Protocol was signed, I was at an international water policy forum in Europe at which an American protested that there was still no concrete, supportable evidence that would lead the u.s. to be concerned about climate change. An Israeli took great exception. "It is one thing," he said, "for Americans to favour out-of-date science, but you ought to go outside now and then." While Americans and Israelis have historically put forward a common foreign policy front on most issues, the relationship between the two was a little on the icy side for a while after that one. This illustrates the fundamental differences in perception related to this very important problem. It also explains why Canadians and Americans have been viewed abroad as blind to their global responsibilities as wealthy countries contributing significantly to a problem the rest of the world has no choice but to address.

When most Canadians think of climate change, if they think about it at all, they can't see why there would be a problem with the world warming up some, especially during the long Canadian winter. As Fred Wrona at the National Water Research Institute once quipped, "Canada is not so much warming up as it is getting a little less cold." What could be wrong with that? Who could object to the Canadian winter being a little less cold?

Beyond being amusing, there is considerable wisdom in Dr. Wrona's joke. Our climate is warming most when the weather is historically the coolest: in winter and at night. It really is getting less cold. It is only when we start thinking about the extent to which our culture has been established and sustained by relative stability in atmospheric temperature that we begin to see the kinds of disruptions warming is beginning to cause. In this, and in all issues relating to landscape and climate change, it is highly instructive to follow the water. When a system as huge as a planetary atmosphere warms up, some interesting things begin to happen and water invariably plays a big role. To begin to grasp the importance of following water as an indicator and measure of the meaning of global warming impacts, it is important to be clear about what is known presently about climate change in our time.

≈

A Climate-Change Primer

WHILE CONTRARIANS AND PUBLIC RELATIONS consultants in the employ of various industry interest groups would have us believe otherwise, there is a great deal we know about climate change that can help us respond adaptively to the problems we have created for ourselves in the Canadian West. Here are ten important things we are sure of:

1. Our climate is a highly sensitive, global telekinetic system.

Telekinesis implies that what happens in one place instantly affects what happens elsewhere. Our climate is telekinetic to the point that small changes in one part of the world can indeed cause dramatic and almost instant changes elsewhere. We know now that our climate is a highly sensitive, global telekinetic system that has taken the better part of our planet's history to evolve. We seldom think telekinetically. Human reactions to our planet's telekinetic sensitivity are local and linear. We will have to think telekinetically and globally if we want to address the climate change challenge.

2. *Glaciations and other climate patterns are cyclical and the influences of these patterns have now been separated from human-induced warming.*

After more than 150 years of speculation and research, we now know that glaciations and a number of other climate patterns are caused by the combined cyclic effect of orbital eccentricity, tilt and planetary precession over time.

In addition to orbital geometry and volcanic eruptions, other geological processes also play a measurable role. These affect climate, certainly, but so do humans. We now know that humans are creating climate impacts that stand out in relief against natural cycles explained by orbital patterns.

3. *Humans may have been affecting climate for a lot longer than we thought.*

We now know that it is possible that humans have been affecting climate since we began forest clearing 8,000 years ago. This impact was accelerated when humans began practising large-scale agriculture some 3,000 years later.

4. *Significant human impact on the composition and dynamics of the Earth's atmosphere began with the Industrial Age and has accelerated to this day.*

Out of the background of orbital, natural and cyclical climate effects, it has become apparent that significant human impact on the composition and dynamics of the Earth's atmosphere began with the Industrial Age and has accelerated to this day.

5. *We may have prevented natural cooling and actually forestalled the beginning of a glacial period.*

It is quite possible that through the emission of large volumes of greenhouse gases over the last century we have actually prevented natural cooling, which may have forestalled the beginning of a glacial period.

6. We have dramatically altered the composition of the Earth's atmosphere, especially in the last 25 years.

We have significantly altered the Earth's atmosphere. It is estimated that in the last century we burned 875 billion barrels of oil. We have dumped half a trillion tonnes of carbon dioxide into the planet's atmosphere in only 25 years. At projected rates of growth, we will add another trillion in the next quarter century.

While there are those who still claim that the atmosphere is simply too big to be affected in any adverse way by human activities, it should be observed that the same was held to be a reason to continue exploiting our oceans, until major fisheries collapsed and marine ecosystems around the world went into serious decline.

Despite those who would wish it otherwise, if you dump a trillion tonnes of greenhouse gases and other pollutants into the Earth's atmospheric soup, you should not be particularly surprised if something happens.

7. Something is happening and it is increasingly measurable.

Something is happening as a result of the amount of greenhouse gas emissions and other atmospheric pollutants we are putting into our atmosphere. Our activities are having a growing impact which is effectively irreversible, at least in the short term. Because planetary systems cannot absorb CO_2 at this rate, the CO_2 we put into the atmosphere over the next 25 years will still be heating the Earth centuries from now. The fear is that ultimately we may find ourselves in the situation of destabilizing or even uncoupling atmospheric dynamics that have taken millions of years to develop.

8. It is not just the direct warming that should concern us, but also feedbacks that exacerbate the impacts of direct warming.

It is not just our direct impacts that we have to understand; it is also their consequences. Our direct impact on climate is small compared to the catastrophic feedbacks we are starting to cause, especially related to the potential large-scale release of methane from the world's oceans, permafrost and peatlands.

It has recently been discovered that huge volumes of methane are frozen into the sediments beneath the oceans in the form of what are called methane clathrates. It is estimated that between 1 and 10 trillion tonnes of methane are tied up in these formations globally.

The release of the methane in these sediments would feed global warming in a dramatic way. But that is the direction we are headed. Since 1955, the planet's oceans have absorbed 20 times more heat than the atmosphere has. At a depth of 200 metres, the Atlantic Ocean has warmed 2°C. Though lasting a shorter time in the atmosphere, methane packs 22 times the greenhouse punch of carbon dioxide.

Similarly, the world's permafrost may encase some 450 billion tonnes of carbon, much of it also in the form of methane. Permafrost is melting worldwide at a rate unprecedented in human existence. There are concerns that we are approaching the point where decay and release of this ice-bound carbon dioxide will outstrip the capacity of growing plants to absorb it.

The impacts are already being observed. In Alaska permafrost has warmed 3°C since the early 1980s. It is interesting that, as of 2003, climate-change-related flooding and erosion had caused damage in 184 of 213, or 86 per cent of all, Alaskan Native villages. A U.S. government report indicated that more than half of these villages may have to be relocated.

Closer to home, a smouldering underground peat fire at the aptly named Burns Bog in the Vancouver suburb of Delta resurfaced yet again in late May of 2007. Recurrent fires in bogs are hard to fight because they are fed by methane released as the temperature in the bog rises. Fires like this have been known to burn for years, demonstrating how such releases can create a vicious circle of higher temperatures which release more greenhouse gases which cause higher and higher temperatures which release even more greenhouse gases.

The fear is that feedback mechanisms of this kind could run away on us globally and warm the Earth's atmosphere very rapidly. This has happened before on Earth, with dramatic consequences. As Fred Pearce pointed out in his book *The Last Generation*, "methane is the gunslinger."

Not counting what is happening now, evidence of 15 mass extinctions appears in the geological record. A mass extinction that took place at the end of the Permian, 251 million years ago, wiped out almost all life on Earth. There is now evidence that the Permian extinction may very well have been a carbon dioxide event. Geologists examining the Permian/Triassic Boundary have found an abundance of fossils that suddenly interface with a life-less black mudstone which, upon analysis, reveals a period during which there was little oxygen as billions of lifeless bodies decayed at the bottom of the sea.

Further research revealed that the catastrophe that caused the great Permian extinction was caused by the explosion of a chain of Siberian volcanoes that introduced enough CO_2 into the atmosphere to heat the oceans sufficiently to force methane out of salt-water solution. The combined temporary impacts of increased atmospheric concentrations of these two gases caused a runaway greenhouse effect that almost eliminated all life on Earth. Geologists are now able to determine the extent of the temperature rise that brought about the loss of 95 per cent of life on this planet.

The sudden temperature rise that occurred in the Permian was in the order of about 6°C, which, interestingly enough, is about the upper limit of the range the UN Intergovernmental Panel on Climate Change has projected for mean annual temperature rise if we do not curb greenhouse emissions in our time.

We can also learn much about greenhouse gas impacts on planetary warming by examining Venus. While much further from the sun than Mercury, Venus's temperature is nearly four times that of the sun's nearest satellite. The reason for this is that the atmosphere of Venus is 96 per cent carbon dioxide. Some scientists believe that the amount of carbon on Venus is roughly equivalent to the amount of carbon on Earth. The only difference between the two planets, according to scientists, is that the carbon on Venus is in the atmosphere while on Earth it is seques-tered in oceans and in ecosystems. This makes a huge difference in terms of surface conditions. One of these planets has water and ideal conditions for life. The other is devoid of life as we know it.

The obvious lesson here is that feedback mechanisms matter.

9. **The world is crowded and natural systems are diminished and fragmented, making adaptation to climate change more difficult than in the past.**

Climate contrarians are fond of saying that the Earth has witnessed all this before and we shouldn't be all that concerned. They are right to the extent that humans have survived through dramatic climate shifts in the past. But the world now is very different than it was when the human population was only a few million mobile and highly adaptable people.

Climate change should concern us because there has never been a time in human history when the ecosystems that provide so many services on our behalf have been so diminished and fragmented. Ecosystem variety and biological diversity, which have historically been the source of natural adaptability, are in measurable decline. A lot of species, such as the mountain caribou in the Rockies, are just at the brink. Global warming, in addition to human impacts on habitat and mortality, could push them over the edge.

10. **We need to know more.**

We need to know a great deal more so that we don't cause unnecessary suffering in our time or make the world less habitable for future generations.

≈

What Warming Does to Water

THE FIRST THING A GENERAL INCREASE in atmospheric temperature does is increase the energy of the atmosphere. A hotter atmosphere means more, and more severe, storms. And storms *are* becoming more severe.

Many wondered, after the hurricane season of 2004, how long it would be before the increasing frequency of extreme weather events would alter human settlement patterns in the Caribbean. As one hurricane-weary Canadian snowbird said after the third major hurricane in a single summer, "What's the point of living in paradise if you have to rebuild your house every second year?"

Then came Hurricane Katrina in 2005. As Joseph Romm pointed out in his book *Hell and High Water*, the devastation in the southern U.S. was almost Biblical in extent. What is interesting is that Katrina had largely spent itself by the time it struck New Orleans. The great damage to the city was largely a result of human failure, not hurricane intensity. We are not prepared for today, let alone for the hurricanes of tomorrow. If Katrina had struck New Orleans at its full Category 5 force, it would likely have resulted in utter destruction. While Katrina could hardly be called a child of global warming, here we saw exactly what the more extreme weather events that are predicted as a consequence of climate change will do to poorly constructed levees and urban infrastructure that is not designed or maintained for such extremes. We also had a graphic demonstration of how environmental impacts can become economic impacts that become social and then political disasters. These, regrettably, are exactly the kinds of problems we should expect to face more often under even the most conservative climate change models.

The weather is becoming more extreme. The hurricane season is starting earlier and lasting longer. It has been calculated that every half-degree rise above 27°C in sea-surface temperature leads to an extra five tropical storms in the Atlantic. Sea-surface temperature is predicted to rise a further 1.1°C by mid-century and 2.2°C by 2100. It is now estimated that storm intensity will rise by half a category on the Saffir-Simpson hurricane scale with the carbon dioxide increases expected early in the 21st century.

It is now projected that hurricane seasons with four or more super-hurricanes — those with sustained winds of 200 km/h or more — will likely be the norm in 20 years. After Severe Tropical Cyclone Monica appeared in the Southern Hemisphere in April of 2006, atmospheric scientists proposed adding a Category 6 to the Saffir-Simpson scale. Monica had maximum sustained winds of 290 km/h.

New Orleans has not been rebuilt. The expense is simply too great, and the U.S. is presently engaged in a costly overseas war. Meanwhile, 19 major American cities and hundreds of smaller towns have been identified as being under threat from the combined impacts of rising sea level and more intense storms.

Insurance companies will no longer provide policies that cover hurricane damage. The increasing damage caused by storms is reducing visits to Florida by snowbirds. Conventions give Miami a miss because of the uncertainty of the weather. Pleasure travel is down. How do you save a city like Miami if you can't save New Orleans?

What would be the cost of infrastructure development to protect a coastal city like Miami from a 1-metre rise in sea level and Category 5 hurricanes every second year? More than we can presently imagine. Some observers have begun to ask if we should be considering abandoning some coastal cities in high active hurricane regions. While we do not have hurricanes in the Canadian West, we are starting to have more frequent and more intense weather events.

A hotter atmosphere doesn't just mean stronger hurricanes and rainstorms; it also means more-intense tornadoes and the appearance of these kinds of storms in places they never occurred before. In 1998 there were a record 1,424 tornadoes in the United States. By 2004 that record stood at 1,817. Now we too are getting tornadoes in places we never imagined. Witness, if you will, recent tornado activity in Canada and warnings that have extended to the eastern Rockies and as far north as the Yukon.

In Canada, extreme weather events that used to occur once in 30 years are now predicted to happen once in three years. Events that happened once a decade are predicted to happen twice a year. Once again, watch what water does. We now know also that a 10 per cent increase in the intensity of rainfall will create a 25 per cent increase in runoff. The same 10 per cent increase in the intensity of rainfall will result in a 24 per cent increase in the erosion this rainfall will cause. Heavier rainfalls cause more flash flooding.

As we saw in Edmonton in 2004 and in Calgary in 2005, stormwater infrastructure in Canada is designed for less intense extremes. The cost to upgrade this infrastructure is beyond our present means.

There are those, of course, who will say that nothing of the sort is happening in Canada. Evidence, however, suggests otherwise. In June of 2005, southern Alberta experienced an extreme weather event that caused extensive flooding in Calgary and a number of neighbouring, rural communities. While the storm was widely regarded as merely a once-in-30-years event, its intensity was of the order we can now expect more frequently as increasing mean temperatures produce more energetic weather.

Perhaps the most interesting part of the storm drama was that in the midst of the flood the city of Calgary had trouble supplying clean, fresh water to its citizens. There was water everywhere, but you couldn't drink it. Clogged with silt and flood debris, the city's water supply system could not keep up with even ordinary demand, and severe water restrictions were imposed until the system could be restored.

When it started to rain again a week later, many communities faced the same problems all over again. By this time it had become apparent that the damage caused by the storm far exceeded anything anyone had imagined. The focus had been on the damage caused in Calgary and in towns such as Okotoks and High River, which was substantial but perhaps nothing compared to what happened in rural areas in the foothills. The total damage to roads, bridges, homes and other infrastructure caused by this single storm exceeded half a billion dollars.

If these are the kinds of storms you can expect to get more frequently with just a half-degree increase in the mean temperature of Alberta, what will be waiting in the wind in a climate three degrees warmer?

It is not just Alberta that is seeing the impact of what weather does to water. Big storms on the West Coast in the fall of 2006 overwhelmed drinking-water treatment systems for more than a month. The storms also disrupted electrical service in Vancouver, Victoria and surrounding areas for weeks, causing some very troubling questions to be asked. How much will it cost to upgrade water treatment and electrical distribution systems so that they will be reliable in the face of annual storms with winds of 100 km/h or more? How do you deal with a more energetic atmosphere and more powerful storms?

What might the appropriate answer to this question be? What does await us in the wind with warmer atmospheric temperatures? And how will it affect us in the mountains?

Water and Fire in the Canadian West

WHAT HAPPENS TO WATER is an important measure of the impacts of landscape and climate change. If we follow what water does and where it goes in the Canadian West, then we will be far more likely to be able to find the way to the West we want.

By managing water carefully while working toward sorting out how we are going to handle global CO_2 and other greenhouse emissions, we buy time. By managing water carefully it may be possible to minimize climate change impacts long enough to allow enough time for our chosen energy innovations and conservation approaches to develop. This, however, will require that we better understand what water is and what water does in our ecosystems and in our economies.

In seeking this understanding, we quickly discover that water is central both to ecosystem and economic function. This link is particularly apparent when we appreciate the extent to which water is married to its diametric and symbolic opposite. Even astute Western Canadians have yet to fully explore the climatic connection between water and fire. There is a fine balance here. If you don't get one, you often get the other. In the West we get big storms, but we also get big droughts. And in the absence of water you get fire.

A higher-energy atmosphere means heavier rainfalls. It also means higher winds. Higher winds topple greater numbers of trees. In the boreal forest this means greater fuel buildup and the potential for more-intense fires. Longer dry periods after earlier peak melt also set the stage for more wildfires.

In 2004, there were already 223 wildfires burning in British Columbia by the 23rd of June. A week later the number of wildfires had leaped to 440, six times the number that had been burning in 2003, one of the most damaging fire seasons in British Columbia history. Though it was only the third week in June, the province had already spent half of its firefighting budget.

As one tired firefighter said on CBC radio, the fire season seems to start earlier every year. He is right. And it lasts longer, too. On Sunday, August 22, 2004, there were 591 wildfires burning in British Columbia. There was a change of weather that weekend which resulted in some 6,500 lightning strikes, mostly in the eastern parts of the province.

Mike Flannigan of Natural Resources Canada is an expert on climate change impacts on our country's forests. Employing two contemporary climate change modelling suites, Flannigan and his colleagues have been able to predict the impacts increased carbon dioxide concentrations will have on the length of the fire season in Canada's boreal forests. This important work suggests that the fire season will increase from 10 days to more like 50 days over much of the Canadian boreal. With a hotter, higher-energy atmosphere, it is logical to expect a greater area of the forest to burn each year. Based on carbon dioxide increases alone, Flannigan and his colleagues predict a whopping 75 to 120 per cent increase in the area burned each year, by the end of the century.

There is so much that remains to be learned. We now know that −40°c winter temperatures are a significant barrier to the northward advance of highly damaging insect pests such as the pine bark beetle. Now that we seldom experience these temperatures anymore, a vast new northern range has opened up to them. Millions of trees from the northern United States to Alaska have been affected by these and other pests. As of 2002 the area through which the pine bark beetles have advanced in British Columbia alone was about 9 million acres, roughly three-quarters of the area of Sweden.

Since 2002 higher winter temperatures caused by global warming continued to aid the advance of this forest pest, which by 2007 infested some 21 million acres of British Columbia forest. Some 411 million cubic feet of commercial wood has been destroyed, double the annual cut of all the logging operations in Canada.

Invasions such as these are almost impossible to stop. It is anticipated that the area of infestation will triple and that 80 per cent of the pine forests in British Columbia will be destroyed. This will mean greater fire hazards, more-intense fires and unpredictable changes to the hydrology of the mountain West.

With wetter, earlier springs, B.C. forests are experiencing explosions in the populations of once-benign species of rusts, fungi and bacteria. Foresters have no idea which species might flourish next as a result of warming winter temperatures and changing hydrological patterns. They can only guess at what ecological disruptions may follow.

We are also unclear about how human impacts on landscapes in concert with changes brought about by increased fire or new infestations caused by forest pests will influence the increasing number of invasive plant and animal species.

The pine bark beetle infestation is the greatest single environmental disaster in the history of British Columbia. It is astonishing how calm everyone seems to be about the impacts. Part of this calm no doubt results from the opening of megamills that generate jobs by processing all the wood available to minimize the economic impact of the infestation. The glut of wood products that will result, however, will likely depress prices. Even with mills running at full capacity, this strategy can only support the province's forest industry temporarily. The real economic cum social cum political problem for the province will come in seven or eight years when there is no more wood to cut and the mills close. When that happens, many rural communities in British Columbia will be dramatically affected. Many simply will not survive.

Many people are concerned about this because they recognize there will be widespread effects on the forest industry and doubled costs for firefighting. Yes, Canada is going to be faced with huge ecologically related economic and social impacts. But again, if you want to know what is really happening, follow the water.

High-temperature fires in particular can change forest hydrology dramatically. The most immediate effect of fire is to destroy the duff layer of vegetation on the ground between trees. This layer, as anyone who has ever walked through a mossy forest after a rain will attest, can absorb up to 1,000 times its own weight in water. This layer releases the water slowly over a long period of time to create the ideal conditions of humidity and soil moisture that perpetuate the forest. The elimination of wildfire in our Western forests over the past century has created fuel buildup which leads to very hot fires. A 1,000°c fire will burn vegetation so hotly that waxy substances in the vaporizing plants enter the soil as a gas and solidify after cooling to form a waxy coating around soil particles.

Though often indistinguishable from other soil layers, this waxy layer will make the soil temporarily hydrophobic. Water cannot pass through such soils, nor can vegetation as easily establish itself to slow runoff. As a result, erosion increases with each extreme weather event and flooding is intensified downstream. Just as importantly, the forest will not retain water for later, gradual release, which ultimately will affect both surface and groundwater flows.

Now that the −40°c thermal wall is falling, we do not know what other diseases and pests will follow in the wake of the pine bark beetle. Nor do we fully understand how fire and water regimes will be impacted by these changes. We do know, however, that the hydrology of the forested regions of British Columbia has already been affected. A study in the Quesnel region in wake of the pine bark beetle infestation revealed that surface flow increased by some 60 per cent on average in areas of total beetle devastation, and by up to 80 per cent where the devastation was followed by rapid harvest of the timber still standing. The result of this is that once-in-20-years floods are now expected to occur in the region every three years. The flooding in central British Columbia in the spring of 2007 is merely a harbinger of what will come next.

We are passing through invisible environmental and economic thresholds we didn't know existed. Even when we spend millions restoring damaged ecosystems, they only rarely return to any semblance of their original states. Can we learn to manage these trends? Will we be able to afford to manage them? Our prosperity will depend on our answers.

These questions underscore the biggest and costliest threat posed by climate change and by our cumulative impacts on the planet's natural ecosystem. Once again we see the extent to which our society has been built on relative climatic stability.

Within the context of that stability, nature provides so many services for us that we would never think to provide ourselves. We are only now beginning to appreciate the extent and range of these services. Think, for example, of what it might cost to build infrastructure to replace the storage function provided in spring and early summer by more rapidly disappearing mountain snowpacks. Think what it would cost to transport water by truck in late summer to places that used to receive it as a matter of natural course.

Water is perhaps the most undervalued and underappreciated of all forest products. Upland forests are the continent's water factories. In many places in Canada we are beginning to realize that water is worth more than wood. One of the principal reasons for the creation of our Western national park system was not to create tourism but to protect the country's most important watersheds. This function will in time become more important than ever.

≈

The Future of Western Watersheds

CLIMATE CHANGE IMPACTS on water availability could alter a
lot of things we presently take for granted. Many communities
will be affected. As long as places with a relative abundance of
water — such as Canmore, Alberta, where I live — still have an
abundance of water, they will be even more desirable places in
which to live and will experience further population pressures.
Though it may be high-end at first and be called something like
"amenity migration," which masks its larger implications, regions
with reliable water sources should expect more people moving to
them. Expect industry to move to these places, too.

As Jim Thorsell of the International Union for the
Conservation of Nature and Natural Resources said at the
International Living Lakes conference at Radium, B.C., in the fall
of 2004, word is getting out worldwide that the Western mountain region of Canada is one of the best remaining places on the
planet to live. Climate warming elsewhere could make where we
live even more desirable to others. The migration is likely to be
what I call IUTW: inland, uphill, toward water. People will come
from all over the world to share in what we have.

They will come from the dry savannah belt around the equator,
from big cities made more vulnerable by climate uncertainty,
from coastal centres in the United States that are no longer as
desirable to live in because of higher summer temperatures
and the frequency of hurricanes, and from the increasingly arid
Great Plains. The influx of outsiders is going to be impossible to
stop. The upland regions of the mountain West are going to end
up crowded. Real estate development will compete with nature,
with industry and with tourism for water. All this is, of course,
predicated on the mountain region having as much water as it
has today. Unfortunately, that is not likely to happen. Town councils and developers throughout the mountain West are planning
communities based on water availability that, in some cases at
least, is not likely to exist in the future.

Some of the economic sectors that are going to be affected by
changing water regimes don't presently know how much they rely

on water to sustain them. Tourism is one industry that needs to be particularly mindful of the impacts that changing water regimes could have on how attractive the West might be to visitors. Canada is a water-based tourism destination. People come from all over the world to experience our lakes, rivers, snow and glaciers. The health of our water regimes is directly tied to our identity as a nation. To this extent, what happens to our water will happen to us.

Snow and ice are central elements in the landscapes and culture of the mountain West. Within this context, it is important to realize how important the presence of glaciers is to this region and what is happening to them.

According to Dr. Hester Jiskoot at the University of Lethbridge, the total area of the 3,271 glaciers in the Canadian Rockies south of 56°N was 4,298 square kilometres in 2004. With just over 1,300 glaciers on the eastern slopes of the Rockies, it can be estimated that the glacier area at the headwaters of Alberta rivers is about 1,100 square kilometres. Dr. Jiskoot indicates that a glacier with an area of only 1 square kilometre has an average discharge of 1 cubic metre of water per second, or about 86.4 million litres per day. The average Canadian uses some 300 litres of water per day, so this single glacier could supply water for 288,000 people each day. However, a glacier doesn't melt for just one day, but for an entire melt season, which is often around 90 days. During that period, a 1 square kilometre glacier will discharge 7.8 billion litres, of water, which would supply about 25 million people for one day or 71,000 people for an entire year. Our mountains really are the water towers of the Canadian West.

From these calculations of average glacier discharge, it can be further estimated that the 1,300 glaciers on the eastern slopes of the Rockies supply approximately 7,776 billion litres of water to rivers flowing into Alberta and beyond. As this is only about 6 per cent of the mean annual natural flow of the province's rivers, maybe we don't need to panic. But before we dismiss glacial recession as an issue, we should examine what the impact of the loss of 6 per cent of current flow might mean in a river basin in which 100 per cent of the existing water is already allocated.

As we all know, statistics can be quite deceiving. We cannot dismiss glacial recession as an issue until we look carefully at when this melt occurs and how it might relate to changes in the timing and amount of precipitation that a warmer atmosphere might bring.

I live next to the Bow River, just outside Banff National Park. In low-flow years, glacial melt supplies 13 per cent of the summer flows at Banff. In extreme lows, up to 55 per cent of the late-summer volume of this river is produced by glacial melt along the Great Divide of the Rockies. The Bow Glacier and the icefield from which it flows are receding at startling rates. Though we act as though we were the first to discover this, the fact of rapid glacial recession has been obvious for a very long time.

Early packer and horse guide Jimmy Simpson, who lived in a cabin on a lake at the headwaters of the Bow, commented 50 years ago on the rapid recession of the glacier. In an interview with Peter and Catharine Whyte on March 30, 1952, Simpson gave the glacier 50 to 100 years before it melted over the horizon. He predicted that other glaciers along the Divide would melt also and that Lake Louise and Bow Lake would become sinkholes. He reckoned that, as a result of the glacial melt, the prairies would have trouble with water supply. Simpson and the Whytes concluded that they were living in the best of times and that they wouldn't want to be around to witness the kind of West that would exist after the glaciers disappeared.

Well, we are around. One quarter of the glacial mass in the cordillera has disappeared in the last century. It is now estimated that at current recession rates the Bow Glacier could melt away within a lifetime. Millions of visitors a year come to Banff National Park and the Canadian Rockies World Heritage Site, adding hugely to the vitality of the local and regional economy. Low flows — or the cessation of flows — of upland watercourses during late summer will affect not just aquatic ecosystem health, but tourism as well. So will the loss of the area's glacial attractions.

These dramatic changes are not just happening on the Bow River. Rapid glacial recession and dramatically lower stream flows have also been recorded at the headwaters and downstream on other important Saskatchewan River Basin tributaries that have their origins in the mountain national parks.

According to Dr. Michael Demuth, one of seven glaciologists working with Natural Resources Canada's National Glaciology Program, melt on the Peyto and Saskatchewan Glaciers presently contributes 45 to 60 per cent of the late-summer flow on the North Saskatchewan in Banff National Park. As the mountain glaciers continue to melt toward oblivion, however, water availability will diminish on the Great Plains. According to Demuth, this will demand a change in the fuel mix for electricity generation. As hydro becomes less reliable, more coal-fired generation will be required, which will likely result in greater greenhouse gas emissions. The kinds of life that inhabit the river will change as the temperature of the water rises due to the diminishing volume of cold water from glacial melt. Aquatic biota should be expected to change dramatically. Eventually, these changes will result in reduced stream flow across the boundary into Saskatchewan.

The prairies supply approximately two-thirds of Canada's $15-billion in annual agricultural exports. According to Dr. David Schindler and his colleagues at the University of Alberta, the conversion of the prairie to agriculture has resulted in a slow degradation of water quality in the basin. While this gradual deterioration must be considered a serious long-term problem, it cannot be separated from the region's history of drought, which will be exacerbated by climate change.

Dr. Schindler has also predicted that human withdrawals in concert with climate change impacts will continue to reduce annual flows in the Athabasca River. Using a climate-based model of stream flow validated by historical data, Schindler and his colleagues predicted changes in water yield in several catchments in the Athabasca Lowlands of northeastern Alberta well into the 21st century. Their model predicted significant declines in total stream flow for each of the catchment areas between April and October. With an average projected warming of 3°C by about 2050, average stream flow reductions were in the range of 8 to 26 per cent in most catchments, with a maximum of 17 to 71 per cent in the warmest and driest years. If the climate continues to warm as expected and stream flows diminish as projected, then the water needs of Alberta's oilsands operations could reach a critical proportion of winter low flows. In other words, water availability in Alberta is likely to limit economic and social development not just in the water-scarce south but also along heavily used watercourses throughout the rapidly growing West.

According to Dr. Schindler, both Alberta and Saskatchewan have already recorded a warming trend of 1°C to 4°C, mostly since 1970. Regional climate models predict that the average temperature will increase by another 4.8°C to 8°C by 2100. This range is outside our society's current willingness or capacity to adapt.

There are also other demands on our water that must be considered when we think about the loss of our glaciers. As the water in so many of our rivers is already fully allocated, even a decline of a few per cent can make a significant difference to the designated recipients of it. Then there is the question of what will happen if, in addition to glacier loss, river flows continue to decline. Flow reductions have been observed in nine major rivers that originate on the eastern slopes of the Rockies. We continue planning for the future based on the assumption that current hydrological regimes will persist. All evidence suggests they will not.

Reduced river flows, reduced glacial-melt contributions and climate-related changes in precipitation patterns and timing are converging to create a new hydrological regime on the eastern slopes and on the prairies. And yet we continue to develop heavily in our headwater regions. We are writing cheques our landscapes may not be able to cash. Instead of learning from the mistakes others have made, we are repeating them.

"Well," you might say, "we can just rely on groundwater." If there is a lesson we have learned from water-scarce areas elsewhere, it is that it is just as unwise to separate surface and groundwater in water management planning as it is to develop inappropriately in your headwaters. As they originate ultimately from a common source, surface and groundwater are simply different expressions of the same supply. When surface water flows decline, it is often only a matter of time before groundwater follows.

Everything in the water cycle is connected. We should be mindful of this when we consider the potential impacts of glacial recession on both surface and groundwater flow. Lower-altitude glaciers throughout the entire West are disappearing at noticeable rates. Climbing routes on Rocky Mountain glaciers are now changing faster than guidebooks can keep up. Many climbers are also observing dramatic changes in the amount of rockfall on many routes as higher temperatures melt the ice that holds broken rock to the mountainsides.

In examining what is happening elsewhere, we observe that glacial recession rates are no longer stable. Consider the unexpected extent of glacial recession that took place over much of the northern hemisphere during the unusually hot summer of 2003. That year, Europe lost a full 10 per cent of its glacial masses during a single hot summer.

We may have lost a similar volume here in the Rockies, but we don't have enough people studying our glaciers to know. As Dr. Shawn Marshall, a glaciologist at the University of Calgary, points out, we have studied only a few of our mountain glaciers in any detail. We don't know how much ice we have, so we can't tell how much we may have lost during any given summer. We do know, however, that Bow Glacier Falls was in full spate in mid-September during the summer of 2003 and the water temperate at the margin of Bow Lake reached 12°C, indicating that a similar degree of loss is likely at least on smaller glaciers.

But there is more to this than just the loss of ancient ice. While the big 2003 melt in Europe was a boon to hydro-power generation in the Alps, nearly half of Europe's nuclear power plants had to shut down because there wasn't enough water in streams not fed by melting glaciers to keep the reactors cool. This might be an object lesson for those proposing nuclear energy development on the already stressed Athabasca River at Fort McMurray in support of further oilsands development.

Some 35,000 people died during the 2003 European heat wave. Wheat production in Eastern Europe that same summer was the lowest it had been in 30 years. Tourism continues to suffer. The Swiss are now wrapping their glaciers in thermal blankets to prevent their loss.

What we learn from this is that it is entirely within the domain of possibility that glacial recession could accelerate beyond current rates. According to Dr. Hester Jiskoot at the University of Lethbridge, climate factors affecting the state of balance of a glacier include air temperature, precipitation and cloudiness. A 1°C temperature rise has the same effect as a 25 per cent decrease in precipitation or a 30 per cent decrease in cloudiness. Each of these influences will cause a glacier to gain less mass.

Scientists studied 12 glaciers worldwide and concluded that, with unchanged precipitation, a rise of 0.1°C per decade would lead to a 10–20 per cent reduction in glacier volume. A rise of 0.4°C per decade would practically eliminate all of the glaciers examined in the study by 2100.

Few people have contemplated what a West without mountain glaciers will be like and what the consequences will be. We just don't know. To find out, however, all we have to do is follow the water.

≈

Adapting to Change

THERE WILL, HOWEVER, ALSO BE BENEFITS connected with climate change in this region – provided the temperature increase is kept within the 2°C mean annual range. Winters will be shorter and, on the whole, milder than in the past. Snow will fall for a shorter part of the year. Spring will come earlier and fall will last longer. Despite the increased presence of fire smoke, there is no question that longer seasons could be a boon to tourism. Though our alpine lakes will lose their spectacular colours as glaciers retreat, the mountain West will remain a beautiful place to live in and visit.

Warmer temperatures and the increased length of the summer season will benefit a broad range of activities. It will likely be possible to begin hiking, biking and camping earlier, especially in the front ranges of the Rockies. The rafting season will start earlier and last longer into the fall, at least while glacial melt continues to augment late-season flow. It will be a pleasure to travel by horse earlier and to enter into the alpine earlier in most years. Taking advantage of these opportunities, however, will demand effective collaborative mechanisms that will help avoid conflict over water use and allocation. More care than ever will have to be taken to protect and conserve water.

As the season of low river flows will last longer, we should expect disputes over who gets water for what purpose. Activities like golf demand a great deal of water. Snow-making for the purpose of ensuring reliable downhill skiing conditions will also become a more intensive water use. In some places, it may no longer be possible to take these activities for granted.

Nowhere is this better understood than in Europe, where it is now predicted that Germany, Austria and Italy will not have reliable permanent winter snow within a decade. Already, ski areas in Europe at less than 1,700 metres in altitude are threatened by the shorter winters and fast spring melt associated with high mean annual temperatures. A good example is the Rhône River Basin, which is similar enough to the Saskatchewan River Basin to be of value as a comparison of potential climate effects.

Climate impact trends in the Rhône Basin are not static. As these trends continue to accelerate over time, the cumulative effects on water will be dramatic. Snow depths in lower-altitude valleys may be reduced as much as 50 per cent annually. In the upper Rhône Basin the snow line is projected to rise by roughly 150 metres for every 1°C increase in mean temperature. The 4°C increase forecast for the region would reduce average winter snow volume in the Swiss Alps by 50 per cent.

Warmer winters will affect ski resorts in the Alps in a number of ways, each of which should be of interest to ski resort operators in Canada. There will be less snow at low altitudes. Snow will melt faster, reducing the number of ski days. The viability of many ski areas — as defined by a snow cover of at least 30 centimetres over a period of at least 100 days — will be greatly reduced. A modest 2°C warming will reduce the reliability of Swiss ski resorts from 85 per cent as in the late 20th century to 63 per cent by mid-century or earlier, particularly at low altitudes.

Snow cover in the Alps has already become more and more uncertain at lower altitudes, as it has in Canada. One of the responses to these climate-related changes in snow pack has been a movement to relocate existing lower-altitude ski resorts — or the ski runs associated with them — to higher terrain. In crowded Europe, however, this movement has resulted in conflict with the protection of remaining natural areas or watersheds. The same problem will present itself in Canada.

As a result of less reliable conditions at low altitude resorts, overcrowding is predicted at high altitude ski areas in Europe. In the lower altitudes, Christmas and Easter holidays will generate less income for ski areas. As well — and this is interesting to us in Canada — the value of on-hill homes and property will diminish at lower altitude resorts. Thousands of seasonal workers will have shorter seasons and reduced income.

According to Dr. Jean-Paul Bravard of l'Université Lumière in Lyon, France, 85 per cent of the 162 ski resorts in the French region of the Rhône Basin were able to extend their ski season in 2002 by producing artificial snow. They did so on 15 per cent of their ski surface between 1,500 and 2,000 metres. The altitude at which snow-making has become necessary, however, continues to rise.

According to Dr. Bravard, the Europeans have also discovered that snow-making can be detrimental to local water resources.

The reasons for this are compound. Because it requires 1 cubic metre of water to make 2 cubic metres of snow, snow-making is highly water intensive. Roughly 4,000 cubic metres of water are required to make enough snow to cover one hectare of ski terrain. By contrast only 1,700 cubic metres are required in Europe to grow one hectare of corn. Thus it requires 2.35 times more water to make snow as it does to grow corn. While in the past this has not been an issue, the higher cost of fossil fuels and the emergence of biofuels as an energy alternative will raise the price of crops that can easily be processed into these products. Giving water away to ski areas may not be deemed as the highest and best use of water resources as fossil fuels become scarcer and therefore more valuable.

Snow-making can demand a great deal of water. Ski areas in the Savory region of the Rhône Basin use the same amount of water in snow-making as a city of 170,000 people. But it is not just the amount of water required for snow-making that is beginning to trouble those charged with managing Europe's watersheds. It is the timing of the requirement. Snow-making always occurs when stream flows are at their comparative lowest.

Because the demand for snow-making occurs during periods of already low river flow, ski areas in the Alps are beginning to compete with themselves and with others for increasingly limited water resources. More than a third of the ski resorts in the French Alps experience shortages of water for their own domestic uses. Water shortages are caused by the fact that snow-making competes with human use in 25 per cent of the ski resorts. In the Alps, half the ski resorts have had to build artificial water tanks to ensure sufficient supplies for both drinking and snow-making.

Europeans have also found that snow-making has measurable impacts on aquatic environments as a result of the strategies they have had to employ to ensure adequate winter water supply. Further withdrawals in winter occur at low flow, stressing the entire aquatic ecosystem of streams and rivers from which the withdrawals are made. Europeans have determined that water withdrawals for snow-making by ski areas are economically important in that they have impacts on water use and resulting productivity downstream. As a result they must be monitored carefully. If you like to ski in Canada, all of these issues are likely already on a menu near you.

The impact of climate warming on ski areas in the Alps has been known for more than a decade. A projected increase of mean annual temperature of 2°C to 3°C by 2050 will have adverse effects that have already begun to happen. Warmer winters will affect ski resorts in a number of ways, each of which should be of interest to ski resort operators in Canada. There will be less snow at low altitudes. Snow will melt faster, reducing the number of ski days. The viability of many ski areas — as defined by a snow cover of at least 30 centimetres over a period of at least 100 days — will be greatly reduced. A modest 2°C warming will reduce the reliability of Swiss ski resorts from 85 per cent in the late 20th century to 63 per cent by mid-century or earlier, particularly at low altitudes. Snow cover in the Alps has already become more and more uncertain at lower altitudes as it has in Canada.

One of the responses to these climate-related changes in snowpack has been a movement to relocate existing lower altitude resorts — or the ski runs associated with them — to higher terrain. In crowded Europe, however, this movement has resulted in conflict with the protection of remaining natural areas or watersheds.

Most Canadian tourism resort planning processes do feasibility assessments based on current conditions and water availability. We are approving expensive resort developments in places where glacial recession, changing rain and snowfall patterns and other environmental factors related to water availability and quality are not fully understood. To protect our investments, we need to know what water is going to do. We need to know more.

What has already happened in the rest of the world in terms of pressure on water resources is beginning to happen also where we live. We are, in fact, a mirror of what is happening globally. In the 20th century, the world's human population has grown fourfold. Urban populations have increased by 13 times. The global economy has grown 12 times larger. Industrial production has increased 40-fold. Energy use has increased 13-fold. Carbon dioxide generation increased by 17 times. Freshwater use during the same period increased ninefold.

Meanwhile, during the same period, the population of Canada has grown sixfold. The population of Saskatchewan has grown 11-fold. While all this was happening, the population of Alberta grew by no less than 44 times. We cannot keep this kind of growth going without severely affecting our water supply.

≈

Water and Our Identity as a People

IN WESTERN CANADA OUR WATER is telling us something. In a single generation, one lifetime, we have gone from a region that was internationally proud of the fact that one could drink from almost any sparking stream, river or lake to a region justifiably concerned about water quality and availability now and in the future.

In every single Canadian community I have visited there are people who are concerned about the decline of the quality of our water resources and are trying to make things better. But wherever there are problems, the problems are always the same. I want to make clear at this point that, in my opinion at least, the enemy is not growth. The enemy is our habit of continuously delaying action on ecological decline until further growth has satisfied what are perceived to be more urgent demands. We know the direction we have to go but there is often a huge gulf between what we should do and what we actually deliver. To create a sustainable society, we need to triumph over the difficulties that obstruct human will to enact changes in the public policy that defines our habits with respect to water use and management. We seem incapable, simply, to act upon what we know.

The Greeks actually coined a word that describes the gulf that often exists between what we know needs to be done and what we actually do; the difference between the decision we need to make, if you will, and the decision we actually render. The word is *akrasia* [ακρασια]. *Akrasia*, according to the Greeks, was "knowing what is right and failing to do it."

Many believe that because Canada is a wealthy country with seemingly endless resources and millions of well-educated people, it is impossible for us to make the mistakes previous civilizations have made in the management of their resources. But our record is hardly perfect.

I invite you to consider the Atlantic cod fiasco. Some of the causes of the Canadian cod fishery collapse have been identified. They include the fact that almost everyone thought the resource inexhaustible; private interests demanded to be served before the real issue was addressed; federal and provincial governments warred over jurisdiction, so no organization could claim charge;

government departments suppressed information; scientists who offered dissenting views were discredited; and short-term political gains were put ahead of the sustainability of the fishery.

An environmental catastrophe became an economic and then a social disaster. The worst thing is that we didn't learn anything from it. Years after a moratorium on fishing was imposed, the stocks still show no sign of recovering. And yet we still allow people to fish.

We literally cannot afford to have this happen with our water resources. We know what is right. We can get over our cultural *akrasia* by going back to basics. And the most basic of all basics is water. Follow the water. The problems we face are not insurmountable. We are not without means. We know how to manage water. The problem is not an absence of knowledge or skill. Nor is growth necessarily the problem. Our biggest problem may be our habit of delaying action on larger environmental cum economic and social concerns until immediate growth has satisfied what are perceived to be more urgent agendas.

We have the collective knowledge and wisdom in our society to become sustainable. We know what is right and, in terms of public policy, we know what we have to do.

We have to acknowledge the importance of our mountain headwaters and be much more careful in how we build in them.

We have to recognize that water is, in its own right, an important forest product.

We have to realize that we are overloading, over-allocating and overusing some of our most important rivers and streams. Talking is great but we have to do something about it besides simply limiting water licences.

We have got to stop acting as though groundwater and surface water are different resources. Groundwater and surface water cannot be managed separately, because their origins are often identical.

We have to build a more functional bridge between science and public understanding and action. We have to invest in more research. We need more data. We urgently need to define how much water we need to keep in streams and rivers to keep aquatic ecosystems functioning.

We are at a crossroads. We have to start conserving water rather than simply looking for more water to waste. We have to take up the slack in our systems through conservation and begin to explore the expanded potential of functioning ecosystems as natural capital.

We already know that our solutions have to be established on a watershed basis. Solutions have to be proactive, not reactive. They have to be multi-agency in dimension and international in scope. We have to take current and projected climate impacts into account in every decision we make about water. Unless we want — in the u.s. tradition — to spend more and more time in court over water issues, we have to develop more proactive mechanisms of solving water quality, allocation and use issues collaboratively. Those same processes will help us address climate adaptation choices.

New monitoring technology and computer systems that can help us a great deal have recently come into existence. Through the use of computer-assisted negotiation and other new tools, diverse interests can work together to craft workable, durable solutions to the most complex water use problems. But we have to start employing these tools. Most importantly, we have to stop taking water for granted. We have to dispel the myth of limitless water abundance in our society. Our culture may be fuelled by petroleum and lubricated by oil, but it runs on water. It is time we realized this.

The most important thing we may wish to do, however, goes beyond simply improving water management practices. We need a new vision in Canada of what we want water to do for us, in our economy and in nature.

The South Saskatchewan River Basin and What We Can Learn from It

THE IDEA OF COMPLETELY REFORMING the way we manage western Canadian rivers is hardly a new one. For me, however, the notion that it was possible to reform our habits in a productive way began with a conversation with Jordi William, a former Minister of Agriculture for Catalonia, who over dinner touched on what is clearly fast becoming a universal problem that ties water to food everywhere. "There is enough water in Spain", he said, "if you reduce inefficiencies in agriculture related to irrigation practices." This particular statement put together all of the arguments I had been hearing in Canada for four years about both the inefficiency of irrigation practices and the resistance to change in the irrigation community.

If it is possible to free up enough water to prevent the limiting of social and economic development in a dry country like Spain by simply improving the efficiency of irrigation agriculture, then surely the same must be true in Canada. Spain also faced, according to Jordi William, the same stubborn resistance to change in its agricultural community that existed in Canada. It follows, then, that the same solution that would work to address the problem of water supply in the dry regions of Alberta would also work in Spain, and vice versa. But what was the solution?

It struck me that part of the answer to this question had already been formulated in Australia. In June of 2006, Paul Perkins from Australia shared a paper he had written on addressing the world water crisis through agricultural reform. As Australia was already facing serious water scarcity, he was beginning to think seriously about how to reframe current resistance to change so that unproductive hand-wringing could be translated into effective action.

Perkins looked at the problem from a different perspective. His goal was to create a different scenario than the one in which Australia found itself so deeply entrenched. His logic in the end was very simple: given the World Bank's assessment of population growth and climate change impacts on world food production, which sees half the world's population water deprived by 2030 but also sees Australia as one of the few regions (along with Canada, the United States, Europe and parts of South America) capable at that time of "water export in the form of cereal grain, meat etc.", would Australia not be more productively engaged if it were to ask the question "how can Australia develop methods to produce twice as much food over 25 years, using, say, half as much water?"

The situation in Canada is different. Climate change impacts, while likely causing dramatic drying on what are now the Great Plains, are likely to improve mid-latitude agricultural productivity. But even so, limits to water supply could hamper this development. So the question Canada might ask may be something like this:

How can Canada develop methods to produce four times as much food for export over the next 25 years, without increasing domestic food prices unreasonably and without upland watershed decline, while still ensuring enough water for environmental services, population growth and proportional industrial and technological development?

Reflecting on Paul Perkins's question and Jordi William's observation, I might propose that part of the answer to how such a solution might emerge is through substantial investment of western Canadian oil royalties in greater agricultural efficiency that does not simply rely on upstream storage development. This investment will be necessary to ensure that individual farmers will not have to cut into already tight margins in order to make their irrigation practices more efficient. Such investment would also ensure that leading-edge irrigation technology and practices emerge that will free up large volumes of water from the agricultural sector that can be employed in specifically directed ways to ensure that water scarcity does not limit the social or economic development of the Canadian West now or in the future.

If we undertook an approach like this, there would also be another advantage. We could export our knowledge and expertise to Spain, Australia, the United States and all the other places that face the same challenge.

Through the United Nations International Year of Fresh Water and other initiatives, it has become clear that to be effective at watershed management, governments need to engage all interests that use or affect water resources. As a result of the development of the Water for Life strategy in Alberta, and related programs in other provinces, the need to link the activities and focus the collective energies of the widest possible range of stakeholders has been identified. Much excellent work has already been done and many excellent examples exist to guide us toward sustainable water use.

By extrapolating what we already know onto the larger landscape, and by borrowing from examples that have worked, it is now possible to imagine revolutionary new ways to employ technologies and advanced collaborative processes already in existence to manage watersheds far more comprehensively than we do today. Perhaps the best place to provide proof of this potential future is in the South Saskatchewan River Basin, since the river is already under considerable stress once its water leaves the mountains.

The South Saskatchewan has its origins in a number of tributary rivers that flow from headwaters in the Rocky Mountains. Agriculture makes the most intensive use of this mountain water in southern Alberta, where vast areas are under irrigation. In order to examine the additional demands irrigation expansion could place on water resources in this region, an important study of irrigation-district water requirements and opportunities was undertaken in 1996. One of the most important results of this study was the development of specialized irrigation water demand computer modelling and data handling tools. Though these tools are remarkable in their own right, the direction they point in with respect to future innovations in water management suggests a possibility of a revolution in how Canadians might work together to address water availability issues in the future.

To understand the nature and potential of the suite of computer modelling and data handling tools presently being employed to increase irrigation efficiency in the South Saskatchewan River Basin in Alberta requires viewing the world from the perspective of a plant in a farmer's field. Imagine a southern Alberta farm located on the prairies, with the Rocky Mountains in the distance. Imagine a plant in that field. Imagine knowing that individual plant's every nutrient need. Imagine being able to continuously anticipate exact parameters of soil moisture, temperature and evapotranspiration and to supply exactly enough water at precisely the right time to maximize growth. Now imagine being able to do this for every plant in that field. Then imagine being able to do this just as effectively and just as selectively for every plant of a different crop in an adjacent field. Imagine being able to do this over an area of 1.3 million acres in 13 irrigation districts that span the width of an entire province. This is exactly what happens today.

Now think on an even larger scale. Imagine knowing where all the water available to you comes from, how much is in each stream and river, how much is diverted for irrigation, how much is used in any given irrigation channel, including how much is being lost to evaporation, how much enters and leaves each water pipeline and each earthen irrigation ditch, and how much is absorbed into the earth as opposed to reaching each plant. Imagine knowing what each plant does with the water it gets in terms of the proportion incorporated into living tissues as opposed to the amount that passes through the plant by way of evapotranspiration.

Imagine knowing exactly how much water evaporates into the air and exactly how much returns to each stream and river, the quality and nature of that water, and what kind of in-stream ecosystem circumstances might be created with the volumes available at any given time.

Imagine what you could know and do if you had such a system. You could literally start with a plant in a field and trace or follow that plant's water needs upstream, past every community or industry drawing from that source, to the headwaters of each stream and river in the watershed to determine how much water was available to grow any given crop within any of the irrigation districts being so monitored.

Imagine also knowing exactly the volume and weight of the water you are exporting when you sell any given crop from any given field, and being able to assign a precise value to the economic benefit derived from any given kind and level of water use. Though there are some limitations, technological advancements are making it possible to monitor an ever-broader spectrum of variables, including water quality at any stage of irrigation and aquatic ecosystem health at any point downstream.

While this is impressive in its own right, the implications of what is currently being done in irrigation agriculture are profound, especially in terms of what it suggests may be possible in the future in the larger watershed and general ecosystem context. By substituting slightly different parameters into the algorithms that drive the irrigation model, broader applications become readily imaginable. It is not science fiction to suggest that the next step may be to expand already existing watershed-based modelling processes to water availability and use patterns in urban, rural and wilderness areas outside irrigation districts. New and relatively inexpensive monitoring systems that do exactly that already exist and are being used in countries such as Spain. Employing such systems in western Canada would make it possible to integrate water management goals throughout an entire watershed in a manner as precise as what has been done in irrigation districts and in some urban centres.

Through application of leading-edge monitoring and modelling tools, it is entirely possible to create monitoring networks that could track how much water was being used at any given point at any given moment in any given watershed. It is possible to know what that water was used for, whether and when it was lost or became polluted, and what its volume and quality were as it entered and left any jurisdiction within the watershed. If this were done in each of the major watersheds and the results extrapolated, it could very well become possible to manage water in a way that will ensure water quality, preserve aquatic ecosystem health, save billions of dollars in unneeded infrastructure costs and maximize the economic development potential of the West for decades to come.

As our knowledge grows, such a system could ultimately be made predictive and adaptive so that it could respond to concerns such as climate change and variability and glacial recession. Such a system could also be made truly collaborative by expanding the watershed management decision-making process to include the broadest spectrum of informed stakeholders. By allowing the widest range of bona fide interests to employ these leading-edge monitoring and modelling tools to input and manipulate actual and potential variables, it would become possible to create a new foundation for effective watershed management.

The advantages of reframing the water availability problem in such a context are numerous. The most obvious advantage is that it transforms a desperate need for change into a virtue. More importantly such a strategy would do a great deal to "climate-change-proof" of one of our country's most vulnerable sectors, namely, agriculture. Such a strategy would also free up water for the environment and for further social and economic development in Alberta and the rest of the downstream Canadian West. The plan could contribute in significant ways to the future, post-energy prosperity of the prairie provinces. We possess all of the technology now to undertake such a project. All that is missing is the leadership and direction.

Two: The Drinking-Water Supply in Canada

≈

What Every Canadian Should Know about Their Drinking-Water

BECAUSE WATER IS ONE OF THE MOST FAMILIAR of all substances, it doesn't usually occur to us that it is also one of the most amazing. If you were to outline the characteristics of water without naming the substance you are describing, it would be very difficult for most people to believe that a single substance could exhibit such a variety of remarkable qualities. Yet we let it run out of the tap without thinking about it. We seldom consider where our water comes from or what has to be done to it to ensure that we can drink it, cook with it or bathe in it without a second thought. Fresh water is also an economic good. Most Canadians have yet to make the connection between how much water we have and use and our prosperous place in the world.

One of the most remarkable qualities of water is that it is perhaps the best example we have of a completely recyclable resource. The water we have now is the same water we have always had since the world as we know it was created. The water that flows across the prairies in the North and South Saskatchewan Rivers, in the Athabasca, the Peace, the Fraser and the Columbia, is the same water that flowed across this continent when the First Peoples appeared. It is the same water that flowed through the Canadian West during the fur trade and through early and later settlement of the prairie provinces and British Columbia. This same water will be flowing down our rivers for our great-grandchildren and their children to use.

Because water is life-giving and because it is finite in abundance and recycles itself through the hydrological cycle of evaporation, rain and snowfall and river and groundwater flow into the world's oceans, water needs to be protected from both natural and human-generated pollutants. Ensuring a clean and reliable supply of drinking-water for current and future generations is deemed an important part of the social contract in Canada and

51

throughout the developed and developing world. Few Canadians, however, fully appreciate how much knowledge, technology, cost and human effort is required to reliably remove contaminants and eliminate unwanted bacteria, viruses and other pathogens from the water that comes out of our taps.

Though Canada has the second-largest volume of available fresh water per capita in the world (only Finland has more), it is not evenly distributed throughout the country. About 60 per cent of our fresh water drains north, while 90 per cent of the population lives within 300 kilometres of the southern border with the United States. In the south, population growth, economic development and dramatically changing land-use patterns are altering hydrological cycles, putting greater pressure on our ability to reliably supply clean water to all Canadians. New and very troubling threats to water quality continue to appear. Moreover, the increasing demand for safe water in many parts of Canada is overwhelming an increasingly aging and unreliable infrastructure. Before we take on the huge challenge and expense of replacing this infrastructure, we need to revamp the way we value and manage water. We need to rebuild outdated water treatment and distribution systems in ways that reflect a different water ethic than the one that has existed in the past. This is a huge project. The creation of this new ethic will require re-education of the public, new attitudes toward managing assets, reliance on non-traditional forms of partnership, and massive public works investment.

≈

How Water Is Managed Today

BECAUSE OF THE WAY GOVERNANCE EVOLVED over time in a large country with a small population, jurisdiction over water quality in Canada is divided in a confusing and increasingly problematic way. Because of the way power is distributed constitutionally, responsibility for the management of water resources is divided between the federal government and the provinces. The federal government is responsible for water quality on federal lands, including First Nations reserves and national parks, and for providing scientific monitoring and advice regarding actual and potential contaminants of water sources. Individual provinces are responsible for the management of water resources and for drinking-water quality in the lands over which they have jurisdiction.

In both federal and provincial cases, jurisdiction over water is most often divided between a great many individual government departments. As many as 18 different federal agencies and, depending on the province, as many as 14 provincial agencies may have jurisdiction over various aspects of water quality and management. Only Manitoba has attempted to unify these diverse accountabilities under a single water stewardship ministry.

Though responsibility for water quality and management is primarily a provincial jurisdiction, both federal and provincial governments are responsible for working together under the terms of the Guidelines for Canadian Drinking Water Quality, published periodically by Health Canada since 1968. The responsibility for the creation and updating of these guidelines falls upon the Federal-Provincial-Territorial Committee on Drinking Water, which is made up of representatives from Health Canada, Environment Canada and each province and territory. These guidelines are meant to comprise a set of standards aimed at assuring that provincial, territorial, municipal and private water users and suppliers are able to protect human health over a lifetime of consumption. The guidelines are meant to apply to both public water distribution and private water supply where individuals rely on groundwater and wells for drinking and other uses.

It is important to note, however, that these guidelines are not legally binding. Provincial or territorial adherence to them is purely voluntary. The standards are no more than they describe themselves to be: just guidelines. Individual provinces and territories are invited to use these federal guidelines as a basis for their own, enforceable standards or regulations. Or they may simply use them as guidelines, as some provinces do. At the time of this writing, only two provinces, Alberta and Nova Scotia, adhere to the recommended federal drinking-water standards.

It is the function of the Committee on Drinking Water to act on new information derived from monitoring or scientific research and emerging circumstances relating to the health impacts of drinking-water contaminants. It is also the committee's duty to update provincial and territorial partners on evolving treatment technologies that will assist them in maintaining and improving water quality. To this end, the committee

lists recommended limits for the presence of harmful substances
or conditions that are known or suspected to affect or threaten
drinking-water quality. For each potentially harmful substance
listed, a limit is determined on the maximum concentration
of the contaminant that may be present in the water before its
quality is deemed compromised. The amount or concentration
is referred to as the "maximum allowable concentration," or, in
bureaucratic parlance, "MAC." Maximum allowable concentration
levels are not set arbitrarily. They are set according to scientific
research findings both in Canada and abroad.

Though university research programs often assist in determining maximum allowable concentrations of water contaminants,
much of the work done in determining water quality threats in
Canada is undertaken by Environment Canada's National Water
Research Institute. This important federal government agency has
research facilities in Ontario, Saskatchewan and British Columbia,
with the largest facility being located in Burlington, Ontario.
Environment Canada's ongoing research is used to define the
current state of water quality in this country in a manner that
allows public policy directions to be put into relief.

The Committee on Drinking Water normally sets maximum
allowable concentration standards for most contaminants at
from 10 to 5,000 times lower than the lowest level at which
adverse health effects have been observed in people or test animals during long-term or repeated exposure to the substance.
While some may feel such standards are excessive, the committee has the responsibility of setting guidelines that will, if applied,
protect all Canadians regardless of age, health or lifestyle. High
proposed standards are set to take into consideration uncertainties in available data relating to potential toxicity and unpredictable cumulative and combined effects of contaminants. These
standards also take into account the fact that some potentially
harmful contaminants may become human health hazards by
way of other means than drinking-water, such as food sources,
environmental exposure or by way of air or other forms of pollution. Constant diligence is required, however, as hundreds of new
chemicals are introduced into the global environment every year.
Most are short-lived and break down with little effect in natural
circumstances. There are inevitably some, however, that over a
prolonged period manifest themselves as new impacts on water

quality in ways that can affect public health. It is also possible that some chemicals, while harmless on their own, become dangerous in combination with other substances.

In addition to identifying the maximum allowable concentration of actual and potential drinking-water contaminants, the Committee on Drinking Water also concerns itself with the appearance, taste and smell of drinking-water. Most often the system works well. For this reason the frequently considerable effort that goes into ensuring clean drinking-water in many provinces usually goes almost completely unnoticed.

While most Canadians hardly think about the state of their drinking-water, threats to its quality are growing nationally in lockstep with population growth and greater industrial and agricultural activity. The national myth of limitless abundance of clean, fresh water is being challenged.

While we are very good in North America at engineering solutions to water availability and quality problems, there is one overriding problem with the way we manage water. That problem resides in the fact that jurisdictions often isolate themselves; rules and regulations are not always followed; the best mechanisms for maintaining and replacing treatment and distribution infrastructure are not always employed; and affected interests do not always share information or collaborate effectively on better water management solutions that are already available that could serve the long-term common good in a more enduring way. Other problems include the rate of population growth, landscape change and climatic impacts on how much water there is and when it is available. These cumulative and combined impacts are now beginning to challenge many of our own assumptions about water quality and availability in Canada.

What Are the Threats to Our Water?

IN JANUARY OF 2001, SCIENTISTS AND MANAGERS at the National Water Research Institute in Burlington, Ontario, organized a major interdepartmental workshop in Toronto at which 45 top scientists examined the state of Canada's water resources. The final report, *Threats to Sources of Drinking Water and*

Aquatic Ecosystem Health in Canada, was published in 2002. The report identified 15 threats to sources of drinking-water and aquatic ecosystem health that Canadians need to understand. Many of these threats have been around since the First Peoples occupied our continent. Others are completely new in that they are products of emerging technologies or the result of cumulative impacts associated with growing populations and our accelerated way of life that have become our societal norm.

1. Waterborne pathogens

Microscopic organisms are often found in even the cleanest water. Some of these organisms don't cause human health problems if they are ingested. Others cause mild symptoms. A number, however, can be fatal, especially if they infect infants, children, the elderly or people with already compromised immune systems.

Waterborne diseases have been plaguing humans since the beginning of time. They became more worrisome after agriculture led to permanent settlement and became an even greater threat to human survival as cities grew in size and complexity. Experience with epidemics of such terrifying diseases as cholera and typhoid have led developed countries like Canada to make careful treatment and management of our water resources a high priority linked directly to the founding social contract of our nation.

As Canadians, we expect to be able to drink our water without getting sick. Over time we have become so good at providing clean, safe drinking-water that many Canadians now take drinking-water quality for granted. We are among the few places in the world that has this luxury. As with all luxuries, reliably clean water comes at considerable cost. Water is a medium of life. Not everything that lives in water, or relies on water, is amicable to human health.

Life on Earth, it appears, has its origins in water and we should not be surprised at the great range of organisms that can be found living in it. By its nature, water is a highly favoured environment for micro-organisms. Only a relatively small proportion of these organisms can be called pathogens. A pathogen is an organism we define as a disease-causing agent in humans. Most of the pathogens that concern us are either bacteria or viruses that flourish in water, but pathogens also include an array of what we call microbes. These comprise a vast array of single-celled organisms that evolved in water long before humans started drinking it. Some of these microbes are responsible for very serious diseases. Despite this, we live very much in association with them. By way of our diverse agricultural, industrial and urban activities, we in fact influence the populations and ranges of these pathogens. We are also sometimes responsible for adding them to the water we later intend to drink.

Sources of pathogens include municipal wastewater effluents, urban runoff, agricultural wastes and, in some cases, wildlife behaviour. Historically, the most common pathogens were bacteria that existed in fecal matter that entered into the drinking-water and into the warm, moist internal environments of people's digestive systems, where they multiplied rapidly. Illness and even death can ensue as a result of the toxins these pathogens generate as a function of their own metabolic processes.

In Canada, the diseases caused by harmful micro-organisms constitute the most common health hazards associated with drinking-water. The presence of these pathogens in our water is the reason why so much is invested municipally, provincially and nationally in high-quality water treatment. Despite these efforts, however, millions of people come down with water-borne diseases in Canada every year. Because the symptoms are usually short-lived and often similar to those of various kinds of flu, the real cause of many of these ailments is not properly identified.

We are very familiar with the kinds of organisms that cause water-borne diseases. In Canada, at present at least, these organisms include bacteria (*Campylobacter, Escherichia coli, Salmonella, Shigella*), protozoa (*Giardia, Cryptosporidium*), viruses and phytoplankton. Each is very different from the others. All can cause serious illness. All need to be removed from water before we drink it.

Bacteria have existed on this planet for billions of years. We now know them as the building blocks of evolution. They remain the most abundant life form on Earth. Bacteria exist in the most extreme planetary conditions, from the hottest to the coldest places on Earth. They are part of the air we breathe, the water we drink, the food we eat and the very ground we walk upon. Bacteria are part of every inch of our skin and are found in every recess of our bodies. They are even found within our very cells. In fact, the number of individual bacteria in our bodies outnumbers our own cells by a factor of ten. If biological classification were based upon a preponderance of cells, *Homo sapiens* might be described as a bacterial ecosystem.

There are more bacteria in our stomachs than there are stars in the sky. The combined weight of bacteria on Earth far exceeds the combined weight of all other living things. We are a life form that has evolved from bacteria and continue to live surrounded and interpenetrated by them. As central shapers of evolution, bacterial history has a direction and a flow. We are witnessing presently only a single moment in this long history.

Whatever direction bacterial evolution will take in the future, water will be part of it. The moment we drink water is the moment at which our evolution crosses paths with the evolution of bacteria. While most bacterial forms are not pathogenic to humans, some can be quite dangerous if found in water. A great deal of science has gone into identifying which bacteria are dangerous to human health and into mechanisms for removing them from large volumes of water quickly, efficiently and cheaply.

One class of bacteria that greatly concerns those charged with safeguarding the quality of our drinking-water in Canada is *Campylobacter*. This particular bacterium is native to North America but was exported to Europe and elsewhere as part of the wholesale exchange of pathogens that occurred through the economic activity and mixing of cultures that followed European contact with the New World.

One species of this bacterial class, *Campylobacter jejuni*, causes a painful inflammation of the stomach and intestine called gastroenteritis. The biggest source of this bacterial hazard as it relates to drinking-water is human and animal wastes. Improperly treated sewage, bird droppings, bacteria picked up by water from livestock wastes on farms or from pet and other wastes that get into water by way of runoff in towns and cities after heavy rainfalls all rank as potentially serious *Campylobacter* sources.

Another bacterium of great concern to those who manage water quality is *Escherichia coli*, or *E. coli* as it is widely known. This bacterium is naturally present in the human intestine, where it most often contributes significantly to efficient digestion. Some forms of it, however, can cause serious gastrointestinal diseases.

When the wrong kinds of *E. coli* find their way into the stomach they can cause an extreme form of diarrhea that can lead to kidney damage or even failure that can lead to death. As many communities in Canada have discovered, one way this form of *E. coli* can end up in the drinking-water supply is by way of improperly treated sewage or through contamination of wells.

Some 2,000 different strains of the bacterium *Salmonella* have been observed to cause diseases of varying severity in humans. While rapid global travel invites the introduction of new disease types at any time, the forms of *Salmonella* that concern us in Canada are presently linked to gastrointestinal ailments which fall under the general classification of botulism. The effects of *Salmonella* infection range from mild flu-like symptoms to severe gastrointestinal infections that can grow in intensity over months as the bacteria releases greater volumes of enzyme by-products that over time turn the body's self-defence mechanism against itself. It is not a pathogen you want in your system.

Shigella is another of the bacterial diseases that existed in North America before European contact that was later communicated to Europe as part of the biological exchange that marked early economic discourse between the Old and New Worlds. It is interesting to note that 40 years ago this disease was the most common water-borne ailment on this continent. It is a measure of our nation's commitment to improved water quality that outbreaks of this disease have been rare in Canada since 1975. Once again, this is a disease that causes painful abdominal cramps and fever. Such symptoms are also commonly associated with microbial infections caused by protozoa.

While bacteria often take the form of tiny rods indistinguishable from one another, or as tiny spheres that are often best distinguished by the mechanisms they employ to procure and process food, protozoa are far easier to identify. They can be loosely defined as single-celled organisms, of which there are many millions that exist naturally in water. Protozoa have been around for billions of years and have become highly adaptive to life within larger host species such as humans. Some of them are very difficult to get rid of once they find their way into our bodies. For that reason, a great deal of effort is made to ensure they do not exist in our drinking-water. Accomplishing this, as we will see later, is not as simple as it sounds.

While most bacterial forms can usually be killed by adding chlorine at some stage in the water treatment process, some protozoa can survive chlorine treatment and must be removed by other means. *Giardia lamblia* is the most common protozoan found in fresh water in Canada. Though it is only peripherally associated with the habitat or behaviour of our national wildlife symbol, this protozoan causes what is commonly called "beaver fever." This gastrointestinal ailment can persist for long periods even with treatment. Though this protozoan contaminant likely has existed for centuries in Canada, its presence has accelerated as more and more people find their way into wilderness areas and as Canadians rely more heavily on private water wells for drinking-water. It is estimated there may be as many as 33 million cases of *Giardia* of one form or another in North America each year. The economic impact of this disease is substantial. Some 150 million lost workdays are attributed to it annually, which translates into a $30-billion annual impact, not including medical costs.

Another protozoan that presents a serious drinking-water contamination threat in Canada is *Cryptosporidium*. This protozoan causes a disease called cryptosporidiosis, which typically expresses itself through diarrhea, stomach cramps and mild fever. Because of its persistence, the disease is particularly dangerous to people who already suffer from weakened immune systems because of other diseases, conditions or age.

Cryptosporidium presents a special water quality challenge in that it is particularly resistant to chlorine. As it can be killed reliably through boiling, the presence of this organism in drinking water is the basis for the great majority of the thousands of "boil water" orders that are issued in Canada each year in areas where more elaborate water treatment processes are not available. But *Cryptosporidium* outbreaks have also — as will be discussed later — created threats to drinking-water quality in some Canadian cities.

Another potential source of serious water contamination are viruses. Smaller even than bacteria, viruses sustain themselves by manipulating the interior function of human cells for their own purposes. Unless you don't mind having your body manipulated by teeming millions of tiny others, it is wise to avoid viral infections.

The most common viruses, such as those that cause millions of colds and flus every winter in Canada, are communicated by droplet infection or by physical contact. There are, however, pathogenic viruses that can be communicated to humans through improperly or incompletely treated water. Among these are the virus that causes hepatitis A and several that can cause gastrointestinal complaints. Not all of these viruses can be killed by chlorine dissolved in water at treatment plants. Some of them attach themselves to sediments suspended in water and can only be removed by very expensive membrane filters through processes which are only now becoming feasible for treating large volumes of water.

These are only the most prominent of a long list of pathogens that have the potential to cause serious health problems in Canadian communities. But even these few make big news. The highest-profile incident involving pathogen contamination in public drinking water was an *E. coli* outbreak in Walkerton, Ontario, in 2001. This tragedy, which became a landmark in the history of water management in Canada, will be discussed later. It should be noted, however, that Walkerton was not the first time in Canadian history that waterborne pathogens have poisoned drinking-water supplies. From 1974 to 1996 there were over 200 outbreaks of infectious diseases in Canada associated with drinking-water. More than 8,000 confirmed cases of illness were reported during these outbreaks. It is estimated, however, that some 10 to 1,000 times more people contracted waterborne diseases but, because of less severe symptoms, did not report them to a doctor. From these numbers it is possible to speculate that as many as 90,000 cases of illness and 90 deaths occur in Canada each year as a result of acute waterborne infections.

We are likely to hear a lot more about pathogens in the future. The National Water Research Institute reported in 2002 that the current status of many pathogen threats to drinking-water and aquatic ecosystems remains uncertain and likely underestimated. The report also pointed to growing concerns about the role waterborne pathogens had not previously been suspected of playing as causative factors in chronic diseases such as ulcers, cancer and heart disease. The message here, obviously, is that we will need to be constantly vigilant in terms of monitoring what is happening in and to the water we intend to drink. But there are other threats besides bacteria, viruses and microbial pathogens.

2. Algal toxins and taste and odour

As flows of some rivers diminish from increased allocation of water resources, and as water temperatures rise as a function of lower flows and higher mean temperatures induced by climate change, an abundance of phytoplankton species are becoming increasingly of concern to those responsible for water quality in many parts of Canada.

Phytoplankton are microscopic blue-green algae that can increase rapidly in number as water temperature in lakes and slow-moving streams rises during the course of a long, hot summer. Phytoplankton numbers can explode to produce "algal blooms," particularly in shallow, nutrient-rich lakes and sloughs such as those found so abundantly on the prairies. The influence of these microscopic organisms can be highly disproportional to their size. Algal blooms in Lake Winnipeg, for example, were already exceeding 6,000 square kilometres in area by the end of summer in the first decade of the 21st century.

Like bacteria, phytoplankton can produce substances that make the water they live in unsafe to drink. Blue-green algae generate what are called cyanotoxins. Some phytoplankton species naturally produce toxins that can have deleterious effects on the human liver and nervous system. When algae populations reach high levels in algal blooms these toxins can be generated in concentrations that are poisonous.

While most Canadians would hardly consider drinking water that has turned green or red with algae, many accidentally ingest algae and their toxins while swimming, canoeing or water-skiing on lakes that are subject to such blooms.

It is often more than water quality that is affected by the presence of huge concentrations of algae in lake or stream water. Phytoplankton blooms are usually an indicator of serious decline in the natural health of an aquatic ecosystem. Their presence suggests problems in the food web within natural aquatic systems and changes in the relative chemical composition of the water. These problems can be reflected in the increased cost and diminished effectiveness of drinking-water treatment. As algal cells and extra-cellular materials can affect coagulation and filtration efficiency in water treatment processes, their presence adds to the difficulties and cost of treating source water to the high standards we need to ensure drinking-water quality in Canada.

Though they occur with increasing frequency and are expected to become more common as mean annual temperatures rise, not a great deal is known about blue-green algal blooms. Their occurrence is thought to be related to nutrient loads, but we still have difficulty predicting just when they will appear. While it is known that algal toxins in stock-watering sources cause illness and weight loss in cattle, the long-term effect of such poisons on human tissues remains unknown. More research is required.

Unfortunately, phytoplankton are now common in many Western Canadian waters and will undoubtedly be of concern in the future to those who manage drinking-water systems and to policy-makers concerned with approaching water-quality issues from the perspective of protecting source water from contamination.

3. Pesticides

Though pesticides are commonly known as toxins, they are unique in that, unlike other toxic chemicals, they are deliberately applied in both natural and artificial environments. There are some 550 pesticide active ingredients currently registered for use in Canada. Some 10 to 15 new pesticides are registered each year. An organization called the Pest Management Regulatory Agency exists to monitor the effects of these new substances and to re-evaluate the impacts of some 400 older pesticides that were registered for use in Canada before 1995.

Perhaps 80 per cent of the pesticides registered in this country are used in agriculture. The remaining 20 per cent are employed in a broad range of applications such as material and wood preservation, lawn and garden care and industrial aquaculture. Policy-makers should know that the toxicological significance of constant human exposure to low levels of pesticides is unknown.

4. Persistent organic pollutants and mercury

Persistent organic pollutants (often referred to as POPs) comprise a group of chemicals that degrade slowly in the environment, accumulate gradually in living tissue and have cumulative toxic properties. Many of these substances evaporate into the air and are thus subject to long-range atmospheric transport. Some, in fact, can be carried thousands of kilometres by the wind and end up impacting places where they were never in use and where they can affect water quality. Many of these pollutants precipitate out in snow or rain and enter water systems to become part of the soil and ultimately part of vegetation. Pesticides included in the category of persistent organic pollutants include such notorious substances as DDT and DDE, aldrin and dieldrin, and toxaphene.

Persistent organic pollutants and mercury are beginning to show up in surprising places. Toxaphene has been measured in relatively high concentrations in the icefield and glacier ice that compose the Rocky Mountain headwaters of the Bow River in Alberta. Between 1975 and 1995, there was a twofold increase in the presence of mercury in thick-billed murre eggs in the Arctic. New compounds such as flame retardants are used in the manufacture of plastics, paints, textiles and electronic devices. Between 1981 and 1999 there was a 65-fold increase in the presence of flame retardants in Lake Ontario gull eggs. This suggests that these chemicals are entering freshwater ecosystems and then accumulating in ever higher concentrations as they advance up the food chain. More, clearly, needs to be known.

5. Endocrine-disrupting substances

Of growing concern internationally is a new environmental risk posed by chemicals that find their way into water that affect the ductless glands that secrete hormones and other substances directly into the blood systems of animals. These are called endocrine- or hormone-disrupting chemicals.

In humans, the hormone-secreting glands most affected by these chemicals include the thyroid, adrenal and pituitary glands. These glands secrete such important substances as growth and development hormones and adrenaline. Scientists around the world are also increasingly concerned about increased human exposure to chemicals that mimic estrogen and other human hormones.

One of the more publicized effects of endocrine-disrupting substances is the so-called "feminization" phenomenon. Though sensationalized by the media, this is not the only effect caused by these chemicals. These chemicals have been found to exist in plastics, pesticides, surfactants and a variety of other modern products. Scientists do not as yet know how serious this threat to water quality and aquatic ecosystem health will become. Presently it is clear only that these chemicals are affecting gender ratios and reproductive capacity of some aquatic species, including fish.

One of the leading experts in this area of water research is Dr. Alice Hontella at the University of Lethbridge. Dr. Hontella has been examining the potential impacts of increased concentrations of endocrine-disrupting chemicals, pharmaceuticals and personal care products in western Canadian streams and rivers. To date, no one knows what will constitute toxic levels or what the combinant effects of these substances might be in terms of aquatic ecosystem health or their cumulative effect on humans. Concerns, however, include the numbers of new products, aging human populations, and effects related to age, sex and diet.

A careful and conscientious scientist, Dr. Hontella does not make exaggerated claims as to the seriousness of this new threat. This is an area of unknowns in which much more research needs to be done. Presently there is no practical, cost-effective mechanism for completely removing endocrine-disrupting substances in the drinking-water treatment and distribution process. This is an issue that Canadians will need to watch.

6. Nitrogen and phosphorus nutrients

Since the 1940s, the amount of available nitrogen has more than doubled. Natural systems contribute some 140 million tonnes of nitrogen to planetary ecosystems each year. Human activities now contribute some 210 million tonnes of nitrogen to that same system annually. In other words, humans create some 50 per cent more nitrogen each year than nature does. A similar situation exists with phosphorus.

Nutrients in the form of agricultural food products flow from farms to the city, where most ultimately end up in landfills as sewage sludge or incinerator ash or in surface or groundwaters. Nitrogen is also released into the atmosphere as industrial emissions and as a by-product of home heating and automotive fuel combustion. Nitrogen released in this way travels around the globe.

The effect of this superabundance of nitrogen and phosphorus is particularly pronounced when these substances are dissolved in water. As the concentration of nitrogen and phosphorus increases in aquatic ecosystems, the resulting dense populations of plants — and phytoplankton — kill animal life by depriving it of oxygen.

Heavy nitrogen and phosphorus loading caused by humans has also resulted in extensive fish kills and increased frequency of toxic algal blooms in Canadian lakes and coastal waters. It has also made clean, tasty and fresh-smelling water expensive to supply in some areas because of the need for treatment to reduce nutrient loads.

7. Aquatic acidification

Acid rain is hardly a new problem in Canada. But though we don't talk about it much any more, it hasn't gone away. Though acid rain had already been identified as a potential ecological stressor as far back as the 19th century, the serious implications of its impact on freshwater resources was not brought to public attention until Scandinavian scientists published research on it in the 1960s. Since then Canada has become a world leader in defining the effects of acid deposition in freshwater ecosystems.

Over the last two decades, both Canada and the U.S. have dramatically reduced their total sulphur dioxide emissions, to 40 per cent less than in 1980. Unfortunately, nitrous oxide emissions have changed relatively little. Research indicates that in southeastern Canada some 76,000 lakes will remain chemically damaged unless additional sulphur dioxide reductions are achieved. Researchers have also indicated we need to know a great deal more about what effects climate change might have on acidification recovery programs in Canada.

8. Ecosystem effects of genetically modified organisms

A genetically modified organism is one that is has been derived not through classical breeding selection techniques, but from recombinant DNA technology, or what is widely known as genetic engineering. Because of global food production needs, this is not a technology that is likely to go away anytime soon. Governments everywhere in the world have been challenged to manage risks and uncertainties that rapidly developing biotechnology may pose to human health and to ecosystem dynamics.

The central difficulty policy-makers face with respect to genetic engineering is that the pace of technological development is taking place far faster than research into impacts can be conducted, and at a rate that far exceeds the ability of slow, cautiously moving governments to establish public policy to manage risks and uncertainties. This process has been made even more complicated by the bitter public debate over the potential impacts of genetically modified foods and other products on human health.

While these debates are important, they obscure the fact that very little is known about the potential effects of introducing genetically modified organisms into our water or into our aquatic and terrestrial ecosystems.

9. Municipal wastewater effluents

In 1996, 74 per cent of Canadians lived in areas serviced by municipal sewer systems. The remaining 26 per cent lived mostly in rural areas where they relied on individual septic tanks or private treatment systems. Of the Canadian population living in urban areas in Canada, 94 per cent were served by at least a primary level of sewage treatment, one of the highest percentages of any country in the world.

Effective wastewater treatment is central to our way of life in Canada. Though we take clean drinking-water for granted, it is one of the qualities of our society that sets us apart from much of the rest of the world. Wastewater treatment, however, is not something we should take for granted. Nor is it something that just anyone should be doing on our behalf. We are putting greater and greater pressure on our water treatment systems. We are flushing more things down the toilet than ever before. We are also dumping things into our water that have not existed before in our water systems. The nature and composition of what runs off our streets, houses and lawns with each rain has also changed.

It has become increasingly important to think about what water picks up and dumps into the storm sewers in each of our towns. Add all these things together and you get the kind of water the sewage plant in your community must treat every day.

Though billions of dollars and some of the most sophisticated engineering have been invested in municipal wastewater treatment in Canada, it is a constant battle to keep up with the kinds of things that appear in our municipal effluents. The National Water Research Institute recommends that wastewater planning be integrated into overall watershed planning everywhere possible in Canada. The idea is that it is easier and far less expensive to treat water that is already relatively clean to drinking-water standards than it is to take out all manner of contaminants that wouldn't be there if we took better care of the places from and through which that water flows to us.

10. Industrial point source discharges

The mining, petrochemical and pulp and paper industries are crucial to the nation's economy. Combined, there are some 1,200 industrial sites in Canada whose production represents approximately 10 per cent of the gross domestic product of the entire country. In addition to this productivity, these industries employ more than a million Canadians. But despite the socioeconomic benefit provided by these industries, effluent discharges from industrial point sources represent a significant long-term threat to water quality, human health and aquatic ecosystem vitality in Canada.

Corporate Knights touts itself as Canada's magazine for responsible business. In its special 2006 national water and pollution issue, *the* publication reported that a total of 115,789,808 kilograms of toxic chemicals were released into Canada's waterways in 2005. This, *Corporate Knights* reported, was up some 5.12 per cent over 2003. The biggest increase in releases was of phosphorus, which rose from approximately 6.5 million kg in 2003, to just under 6.9 million kg in 2005. The article also pointed out that had it not been for just two pulp and paper facilities that increased phosphorus releases by a combined half million kilograms in only two years, there would actually have been a substantial national decrease. But other point source concerns also exist.

There are new drinking-water quality challenges emerging that relate to the extent and impact of our search for hydrocarbons, particularly in Western Canada. These include problems associated with deep-well injection to optimize oil field recovery, and growing concern over potential effects on groundwater quality and availability brought about by coalbed methane and related extraction processes. There is also a great deal of concern about the potential long-term consequences of major resource development projects such as oilsands.

These are hardly minor concerns, especially if you rely on subsurface aquifers for drinking-water in areas being exploited for petroleum resources. A 2002 report by the Canadian Council of Environment Ministers put forward what we know and don't know about the effect of petroleum extraction on groundwater resources. The report noted that, as part of coalbed methane operations, large volumes of water of marginal chemical quality is often brought to the surface. "The impact of disposing of these volumes of water at the surface or in the near subsurface in Canadian environments is totally unknown," the report said. It went on to indicate that knowledge borrowed from u.s. sites with different climate and soil types was "often less than ideal." The report also pointed out that "aging field, production and refining facilities, flare-pits, drilling sumps, improperly abandoned bore-holes, past spills, and aging subsurface infrastructure" were already known sources of groundwater contamination.

The report went on to identify what was not known about long-term petroleum-related impacts on groundwater in the Canadian West. The list included the long-term integrity of pipelines, exploration borehole seals, and abandoned-well cement plugs and steel casing. The report also indicated that little was known about the potential impact or the scale of groundwater contamination should wells in an old field start failing.

The report concluded by observing that missing groundwater data had to be filled in and long-term impacts understood. In conclusion, the report recommended that "approval of non-conventional energy developments and development in frontier areas without adequate baseline groundwater knowledge may have unintended future consequences, affecting groundwater quality on a regional scale."

At the time of writing, coalbed methane extraction remains a very controversial issue in many areas of Western Canada. The petroleum industry is anxious to develop subsurface resources while natural gas prices are high. The people who live in rural areas affected by this kind of development are concerned for very personal reasons. Groundwater data collection and interpretation has been inadequate or non-existent in many areas, because such programs are often cut when provincial governments reduce budgets. Most landowners, on the other hand, monitor their wells daily, both formally and informally. Though not always highly scientific in their methodologies, they have been measuring, often for a lifetime, the one single standard that matters the most to them: can they drink the water and can their livestock drink it?

Many people now argue that the past lack of continuous investment in monitoring and the research necessary to fully understand the extent, nature and state of groundwater resources in the western provinces is becoming a barrier to economic development. Just when the oil industry is pressing for rapid development of coalbed and other unconventional energy opportunities, the government agencies responsible for groundwater protection find themselves unable to supply the information required to give landowners and others the comfort they need to accept industry terms.

While leaders in the oil industry are attempting to give farmers and ranchers the assurance they need that the long-term quality of their water will be protected, there is still a great deal of doubt. Telling a rancher that noticeable changes in the quality of the water he has been drinking for 50 years — changes that occurred at the exact time coalbed methane activity was initiated in his area — can't possibly be a consequence of that activity is not the best way to make friends. Anytime you get an engineer behind a computer screen in an office tower telling farmers or ranchers who has been on their land for decades not to believe what they are seeing right in front of their own eyes, you create a foundation for mistrust.

Until knowledge of groundwater availability and dynamics and protection policies catch up to extraction policies, coalbed methane and related issues will be hard to resolve.

Another issue related to point source contamination of water in western Canada relates to oilsands development. Presently tar sand refinement processes generate large volumes of heavily contaminated water that no one knows yet how to properly treat in a timely manner. Vast tailings ponds are accumulating, waiting for a more satisfactory solution to the contamination problem. An accidental failure of one of these ponds resulting in a major release into the neighbouring Athabasca River would create more than a drinking-water problem. It would create an environmental disaster of continental proportions. As one expert observer pointed out, "Alberta has a Bhopal in the making, and it should not be waiting to do something about it."

11. Urban runoff

About 80 per cent of all Canadians, some 25 million people, live in urban areas. Cities are not always ideal places for water to purify itself. Rainfall and snowmelt are converted into urban runoff. This runoff is transported by sewers, drainage channels and streams and ultimately discharged into receiving waters in one of two ways. In urban areas serviced by storm sewers this water pours somewhere downstream into a river, a lake or the ocean. In new urban developments, some mitigation of flooding and erosion has been achieved in the past 25 years through enhanced stormwater management practices. The long-term performance of new stormwater management facilities, however, remains uncertain. In older areas, where retrofitting of systems is the only practical option, hardly any progress has been made in controlling the impacts of runoff.

Cities facing pollution problems associated with urban runoff include Vancouver, Edmonton, Winnipeg, Hamilton, Toronto, Ottawa, Montreal, Quebec City and Halifax.

All of these problems are expected to become more complicated as climate change brings about greater variability in weather and more frequent and more intense weather events that severely stress infrastructure which most often has been designed for less frequent and intense extremes.

12. Landfills and waste disposal

Wastes are part of human life. Wastes are produced in every human endeavour in our society, in everything from domestic, commercial and industrial to agricultural activities. In Canada, these wastes are recycled, incinerated or treated or simply disposed of in landfill sites.

The approaches to disposal range from highly sophisticated waste management operations to simple landfilling and spreading operations to deep-well injection. While surface water contamination occurs as a result of direct runoff from waste sites to streams, lakes and wetlands, the main threat posed by solid and other wastes is the effect that improper disposal can have on groundwater.

The dynamics of groundwater contamination are very different from those of pollution of surface waters. Because we cannot observe groundwater, we typically discover it is contaminated only when we discover contamination in a well or surface water body connected to that groundwater system. Groundwater contamination may commence decades or even centuries after the waste source is in place. The slow release rate can cause pollutants to take thousands of years to move through groundwater flow regimes. As a result, groundwater contamination can be difficult if not impossible to remediate.

As the good people in Elmira and Smithville, Ontario, Abbotsford, British Columbia, and Ville Mercier, Quebec, have learned, groundwater contamination can damage drinking-water supplies for centuries to come. As our wastes continue to build and our population continues to grow, we should expect more frequent — and persistent — groundwater contamination surprises. We should appreciate that it is invariably cheaper and easier to prevent groundwater contamination than it is to attempt to repair damage to water supplies once it occurs.

13. Agricultural and forestry land use impacts

Canada is one of the world's largest exporters of forest products. Though almost unimaginable by world standards, the area of Canada presently actively managed for timber harvest represents only a fraction of what could be logged in the future. About 59 per cent of Canada's forestlands, some 245 million hectares, are capable of producing commercially valuable timber.

Timber harvesting, however, does affect water regimes. Changes in soil characteristics and forest hydrology that accompany logging have raised concerns about the quantity and quality of water supply to nearby lakes, streams and wetlands. Also of concern are the effects that changes in water quantity and quality have on aquatic organisms and ecosystems.

Over the last half century there has been a Green Revolution in Canadian agriculture. Food shortages in many parts of the world have been alleviated, temporarily at least, by the introduction of new crop varieties that resist disease, maximize yield and facilitate multiple cropping. Canada is a leader in these applications. The achievement of full yield potential, however, demands dramatically increased use of chemical nutrients and pesticides. Fertilizer use in Canada over the last 50 years has increased nine-fold. The use of pesticides has increased by 32 times. What is spread on crops enters our water and can generate nutrient loading that induces phytoplankton activity and other problems.

14. Natural sources of trace element contaminants

Not all the threats to water quality and aquatic ecosystem health in Canada are posed by human activities. Some sources of trace contaminants exist naturally as part of the Earth's surface geology.

Mapping of the geologic sources of natural contaminants has been ongoing in Canada for decades, but is far from complete.

15. Impacts of dams/diversions and climate change

Most of Canada's 600-odd large dams store water during peak flow periods and release it to provide water and generate electrical power during winter low-flow periods. Research has proven that changes in water quantity alter its quality both within the reservoir and downstream. Low flows alternating with sudden releases of large volumes of water cause considerable stress on downstream aquatic ecosystems. These unavoidable impacts will be intensified as the Canadian climate continues to change.

Why Threats to Canadian Water Quality Matter: Lessons from Walkerton, Ontario

SOME OF THE THREATS OUTLINED in the National Water Research Institute reports have been with us for some time. Others are only beginning to emerge. All of these threats, however, will require action if the quality of Canada's drinking-water is to be protected and improved. Unfortunately, the atomized jurisdictional and monitoring mechanisms by which we attempt to ensure drinking-water quality over the long term are outdated and may no longer be adequate for many of the problems we are creating for ourselves in the management of water in Canada. This was proven beyond any doubt at the turn of the millennium by a terrible tragedy that befell the town of Walkerton, Ontario.

Wholesale contamination of urban water supplies in North America is not a new phenomenon. System failures in the 1990s severely tested public confidence in their drinking-water supply in a number of American cities. Journalist Sara Terry told the story very completely in "Drinking Water Comes to a Boil," an article she published about water-quality catastrophes in Milwaukee and elsewhere in the September 26, 1993, edition of *The New York Times Magazine*. It was on the night of April 7 of that year that Mayor John Norquist of Milwaukee realized he had a water contamination problem of epidemic proportions in his city.

For several days before, there had been growing complaints among citizens of stomach pains and diarrhea. That night, the mayor was called away from a ceremony at the Police Academy by worried health officials. The city had eight confirmed cases of cryptosporidiosis and the water supply appeared to be the most likely source of contamination.

For Mayor Norquist, the city's reputation hung on whether it was necessary to issue a boil water advisory for almost a million residents served by the public water system. It was not an easy decision. As Sara Terry reported, a big u.s. city would make the news around the world if it were, in effect, to declare that its water supply system was contaminated by the pathogens that were common only in the developing world. While some officials urged the mayor to wait for more definitive evidence that the source of the pathogen was the water supply, Norquist wasn't sure it was wise to wait. Looking around the table, the mayor noticed that the state epidemiologist, Jeffrey Davis, was drinking a can of soda. When asked if he would drink the city's water, Davis declined the offer. "Well, if you don't want to drink it," said the mayor, "I don't think anybody in the city of Milwaukee should drink it. I've got all the evidence I need."

The boil water order was too late to prevent serious health problems in the city. The *Cryptosporidium* parasite sickened 406,000 residents. Some 4,000 people were hospitalized and 111 died in what became the largest recorded outbreak of water-borne disease in United States history. In July of that same year, the city of New York experienced a similar contamination. Though no illnesses were conclusively linked to the contamination, these combined events forced the Environmental Protection Agency in the United States to set safer levels for several dozen contaminants present in drinking-water and ensure that state authorities enforced those standards.

While most of the public attention relating to water-quality issues was focused on the disaster in Milwaukee, Canada was lining up to have very similar problems of its own. Across the border, the shortcomings of Ontario's drinking-water systems had been known for a decade. In 1992, a report by the Ministry of Environment & Energy indicated that fewer than half the water treatment plants in the province complied with existing provincial health parameters. In 1993, a *Cryptosporidium* outbreak similar to the one that killed 111 people in Milwaukee sickened almost 24,000 households in the Kitchener-Waterloo area. After a similar outbreak in Collingwood, Ontario, in 1996, the provincial government declared that 43 of the water treatment facilities it operated were vulnerable to the same form of contamination. Despite the warnings, no one was prepared for what happened next.

In May of 2000, an outbreak of *E. coli* O157:H7 and *Campylobacter jejuni* killed seven people and sickened 2,300 others in the small town of Walkerton, Ontario. To this day there are some 150 people who have not, and probably will not, recover from the effects of the illness the outbreak brought in its wake. The economic costs caused by this outbreak were measured at $150-million. There were also incalculable psychological costs. A political shock wave originating in that event continues to reverberate across the country.

The immediate cause of the outbreak was a once-in-60-years heavy rainfall that caused the town's water source to be contaminated. In essence, an extreme weather event overwhelmed the integrity and safety of the community's water treatment infrastructure and operations. (It should be noted that extreme weather events of this nature are expected to occur with greater frequency under all climate change scenarios produced for Canada.)

The first problem was that one of the town's wells was not in proper working order. The problem of the failed well was exacerbated by the employment of complacent and deceitful staff in key roles associated with management of the town's water system. These two problems were compounded by the fact that there was no automatic shutdown mechanism that would prevent contamination from spreading once the system had been overwhelmed.

These problems were further exacerbated by inadequate inspection and the failure of provincial and municipal oversight. The risks associated with the failure of the water supply system were not communicated internally or externally. In sum, there was a complete absence of proper management process which caused the water supply system in Walkerton to fail to function safely the moment it was stressed by an extreme weather event of the kind that is projected to become more common as our climate in Canada changes. But later investigations pointed out that there was more to this catastrophe than simple local incompetence and a chain of unfortunate failures.* [**Please see note at foot of next page.**]

In summarizing his analysis of the tragedy, Justice Dennis O'Connor of the Court of Appeal for Ontario pointed out that while technical advancements in water treatment have been very effective in delivering high-quality drinking-water to Canadians, no legally enforceable standards exist in Canada today. In fact, the only standards that existed at the time of the Walkerton failure had been created in 1976 and were inadequate and largely unpoliced.

Another careful observer of the Walkerton catastrophe is Harry Swain, an experienced retired politician who analyzed the public-policy implications of the disaster. Swain has observed that gaps in knowledge caused by the fact that baseline data collection relating to water quality and availability are usually among the first budget items to be dropped when governments need money for other things. Swain claimed in 2006 that the federal government still hadn't caught up to the lessons that ought to be learned from Walkerton. The only places for which policy had been developed by the federal government at the time of this writing were Indian reserves, military installations and national parks. Despite double the spending, three-quarters of the Indian reserves in Ontario alone still operated unsound water supply systems and no legally enforceable federal standards existed anywhere in Canada.

Among Justice O'Connor's principal recommendations was recognition of the central importance of source protection as a means of ensuring water quality in Canadian communities. It was held almost universally among parties of standing that it is cheaper and safer to start with clean water at the outset of the water treatment process than it is to manage contamination. Licensing and accreditation of water providers was also seen as central in efforts to ensure that what happened in Walkerton doesn't happen again. In this broad category of recommendations many important elements were identified as being in need of improvement. These included more comprehensive training

---

* Formal government reports relating to the Walkerton fiasco do not give the full impression of what happened in that very pleasant community during this crisis. For a very compelling interpretation of how a crisis of this kind can divide a community against itself and how much suffering water contamination can cause, the reader is invited to view the 89-minute, made-for-television drama *Betrayed*, produced by CBC television in 2003. The video is available through the CBC or from selected video stores.

of water supply technicians, better laboratory processes, higher
and more universally monitored standards, more effective federal
leadership in water quality and management issues and a measurable improvement in performance and accountability at all levels
of government.

The findings of the Walkerton inquiry are far-reaching. It
is clear there is missing science that we need to undertake
in Canada, especially in hydrogeology. More refined risk
assessments are required for drinking-water quality standards.
Walkerton teaches us that, in terms of effective management, the
tools are well known, but they are of little use to us if we do not
use them. Canadians know all about "total quality management"
systems, training and certification. We know how to create laws
that establish the appropriate standards of care, and we have
to enforce those laws. Unless we do, however, Walkerton will
happen again and again.

Perhaps the most important lesson learned from Walkerton
has to do with the current state of water treatment and delivery
infrastructure renewal in Canada. It is estimated that 85 per cent
of the water utilities in Ontario alone are too small to be safe and
efficient. If that is the case in wealthy Ontario, what is the state of
water infrastructure elsewhere?

The Walkerton fiasco woke Canadians up to just how easy
it is for things to go quickly and seriously wrong with complex
water supply systems. Many water-quality professionals think
Walkerton was just the tip of the iceberg. They cite scores of other
communities in which water-quality issues could surface as serious local health threats. Unfortunately, this appears to be exactly
what is happening.

In 2001, a *Cryptosporidium* outbreak endangered the health
of 7,000 residents in North Battleford, Saskatchewan. Despite
federal oversight, Walkerton is repeating itself annually on federal lands designated as First Nations reserves. But it is not just
on reserves that Canadians are beginning to confront serious
drinking-water-quality issues. Each year, hundreds of Canadian
municipalities have to issue boil water advisories because of
the existence of or the threat of contaminated water. British
Columbia issues some 500 such advisories a year, more than any
other province. In Alberta, health authorities issued 123 advisories between 2002 and 2004. Poor water quality bears a high

social and economic cost. Health problems related to water pollution in general cost Canadians an estimated $300-million per year.

This data demonstrates that there can be a huge gap in the quality of services that supply drinking-water to rural and urban Canadians. It also points to significant problems in the future with respect to the infrastructure we have created in this country to ensure the reliable delivery of safe water.

≈

Ensuring Reliable Supply of Clean Drinking-Water in Canada

THE QUESTION OF WHERE YOUR WATER comes from will depend on where you live. While many Canadians rely on local wells to supply drinking-water, most, especially in urban areas, get their water from public utilities. Public utilities are government agencies or companies that are responsible for the supply of valuable common necessities such as electricity, natural gas or water to the public. While most utilities specialize in the supply of one or the other of these essential services, some private-sector utilities are able to supply both electricity and water to their customers.

Utilities may draw the water they provide for their customers from a surface water source such as a nearby river or lake or from groundwater sources such as subsurface aquifers. In many places, utilities draw the water they need from both surface and groundwater sources. In order to ensure that the water they supply is of the highest quality, most utilities disinfect it to ensure that it does not contain viruses, bacteria, protozoa, parasites, phytoplankton or dissolved chemical contaminants that could affect the health of a person drinking it.

The process by which water is purified so that it will be safe to drink is called water treatment. As has already been explained, there are a number of ways in which water can be contaminated as it is moved from its source to our taps, and water treatment must respond to each hazard. Groundwater may flow through sulphur-, zinc- or arsenic-laden geological formations before it is collected for use. Groundwater can also pick up contamination from fertilizers, septic tanks, mine drainage or naturally occurring minerals. Contaminants carried from elsewhere can fall in rain or snow. Rivers and streams sometimes carry harmful micro-organisms that find their way into water from domestic livestock, wildlife or humans. Storm drains can carry contaminated runoff from cities into rivers and streams. Other potential sources of pollution include landfills, where rainwater can soak into the ground and leach out harmful substances, transporting them into groundwater. Pollutants and contaminants can also enter water supplies from farm drainage and even from sewage treatment plants themselves. In homes, factories and buildings, corrosive water can dissolve lead in water pipes. You can pick up contaminants from an improperly washed glass or cup.

Some pollutants increase the turbidity of water and thereby reduce its clarity. While turbidity was once considered to be of æsthetic interest only, it is now viewed as a serious water treatment concern, as particles suspended in water are now known to harbour and shield disease-carrying micro-organisms and allow them to escape the effects of disinfection. For this reason, complete water treatment includes a number of steps to ensure that pathogenic micro-organisms have been reduced or removed from the water before it is transported through the distribution system as drinking-water.

While individual users in rural areas and small communities may employ a variety of mechanisms for ensuring clean drinking-water, most large cities in the world follow the same seven basic steps to maintain water quality for their citizens. As initial quality and ultimate standards for drinking-water may vary from region to region, utilities will sometimes focus more on some of these steps than on others. What is important about these steps is that they work, and most often they do. Water quality is not something many Canadians think about. Water treatment plants and distribution networks reliably supply clean, safe drinking-water to millions of people a year. Most of the people who enjoy the benefits of this water would be hard pressed to name even one of the steps in the elaborate but very reliable and cost-efficient process that makes it available to them.

Step one: Capture and system intake

The water to be treated for drinking and other uses such as washing, bathing and cooking has to be captured from a natural source or from a waterworks built for this purpose. In most cases, surface water is captured and then piped or pumped from a nearby water source into the wastewater treatment facility. Initial screening is done at this first stage to prevent large objects such as floating garbage, branches and logs from entering the treatment process. This screen is also designed to keep living things such as fish from entering the system.

In cases where groundwater is the source, filtering is usually less complicated, as most of what might be suspended in the water may already have been filtered out by the soil and rock through which the water has flowed to reach the treatment intake. There are many cases in which groundwater sources are so pure they require little, if any, treatment. These situations are increasingly rare, but where they do exist, they speak to water treatment cost savings that can accrue through the careful protection of water sources and upland watersheds.

Step two: Add chemicals to kill bacteria and improve taste

Chlorine, which is used in 98 per cent of all Canadian water treatment plants, is the most commonly used of all water treatment disinfectants. The reason for this is that chlorine is very effective at killing most bacteria that can be found coming into domestic treatment plants. Chlorine also causes suspended particles in the water to coalesce and settle out so that bacteria hiding in these sediments can be killed or removed.

Chlorine is inexpensive to make and use and has the added advantage of remaining active and effective not just in the initial treatment but all along the way as it accompanies the treated water through the distribution system to homes and businesses in the communities served by the treatment plant. Because of chlorine, and chlorine-like substances, an entire drinking-water system can remain relatively free of harmful bacteria right from the plant to where the water flows out of our taps and into our kitchen sink or bathtub.

There are, however, some aspects of chlorine that, depending on the nature of the water being treated, can under certain circumstances cause the formation of by-products that may be harmful to human health. These by-products have been discovered to be far more numerous than anyone anticipated. This concern has led to the development of alternative and additional regimes of chemical and physical treatment, which we will discuss later.

Step three: Coagulation and flocculation

Killing bacteria is only the first step in ensuring clean drinking-water. For almost a century, chemicals such as chlorine and aluminum sulphate, also known as alum, have been mixed into the water at treatment plants in Canada to kill bacteria. Aluminum sulphate and other chemicals also have the power to cause suspended sediments floating on or in the water to be drawn together in such a way that they clot or curdle and then solidify. The products today are known by trade names such as NIAD or ISOPAC. These products help coagulate sediments in which bacteria like to hide.

These loosely massed sedimentary clusters often resemble tufts of wool and are called floc. Flocculation is the process of concentrating sediments in water into masses of floc and then causing them to sink from the water so they can be removed. As well as contributing to disinfection, this process reduces turbidity in the water, which adds considerably to both appearance and quality.

Step four: Sedimentation

After the addition of chemicals that induce coagulation and flocculation, the water in a treatment plant usually flows into a sedimentary basin where it is allowed to sit long enough to allow the floc to settle to the bottom. Interestingly enough, it is not just the floc and what it already contains that settles out of the water at this stage: bacteria remaining in the water actually gravitate to the floc and attach themselves to the woolly tufts and are drawn out of the water when the tufts settle to the bottom of the sedimentary basin.

Step five: Filtration

In most large-scale water treatment facilities, the next stage of treatment involves squeezing the water through filters to ensure that any remaining particles are removed. The materials employed in this filtration process can include layers of sand or gravel or even porous coal or other forms of activated carbon capable of removing the smallest remaining sediments or floc.

Step six: Final disinfection

After filtration, the treated water is transported to storage facilities, which are sometimes called clear wells, or enters directly into the distribution system. En route, this water is often treated a final time with small amounts of chlorine or similar chemicals so as to kill any bacteria that may have survived previous steps of the process. Enough chlorine is put into the water to ensure that any new bacteria entering the distribution system before the water reaches people's homes or businesses are also killed.

Step seven: Distributing the treated water

In order to ensure the treatment system is working properly at every stage in the process, samples are taken and carefully examined to ensure that the water is safe to drink as it enters the distribution system.

As water is heavy and often very expensive to pump, holding tanks are generally built on high ground. (It is for this reason that water towers were once so common in many Canadian communities.) Distribution systems are generally composed of a series of large pipes, or mains, which connect to smaller and smaller systems until the water reaches individual homes and businesses.

In today's highly efficient world, the volume of flow permitted through any given water main is likely to be carefully controlled by computers that balance distribution over vast areas. Just as treated water is tested to ensure its quality throughout the treatment process, in most areas it is also tested as it flows through distribution channels on its way to its final destination. In some large distribution systems, additional chlorine or other chemicals can be added at established points to ensure that no new bacterial sources affect water quality.

Properly operated and monitored, the water treatment process works very well, supplying clean, fresh water to millions of people in Canada every year. We have discovered, however, that constant diligence is necessary with these systems, and that evolving improvements are required to ensure that operational problems can be overcome as they emerge.

Improvements to the
Basic Drinking-Water Treatment Process

THE DEVELOPMENT OF FUNCTIONAL, EFFECTIVE and cost-efficient water treatment processes was a major landmark in public health in Canada. Through a century-long effort involving microbiologists, engineers, public health administrators and federal and provincial government agencies, serious waterborne diseases such as cholera and typhoid fever are no longer a threat to Canadians. Because of careful water treatment, these diseases are uncommon in Canada today.

This public health breakthrough, however, has not come without cost. Though it is clear that modern water treatment methods are very effective, there has been concern about the health implications of prolonged exposure to some of the chemicals that are used in our current drinking-water treatment processes. Concerns are principally focused on the long-term effects of adding such chemicals as chlorine, aluminum and fluoride to our water supply. These concerns have led to some interesting and innovative new approaches to making our drinking-water safer.

The main dilemma in water treatment revolves around the kinds of chemicals that are best suited for disinfection. Chlorine works very well in most water treatment situations. Only when it is added as a disinfectant to water that has a high concentration of natural organic materials or residues does it produce problems. Natural organic materials enter natural water systems primarily through decaying vegetation and biological production from surrounding ecosystems. These compounds will vary dramatically in nature depending on whether the source water for treatment flows through a deciduous or coniferous forest or a prairie, or through urbanized environments that generate their own completely unique combination of organic materials. Organic substances that cause chlorine-based reactions include decayed leaves and human and animal wastes — just the substances that chlorine is employed against in the water treatment process. Each of these different kinds of material will generate its own specific disinfection by-products.

In interaction with these substances, chlorine produces more than 500 kinds of disinfection by-products. These by-products arise when chlorine breaks down the walls of organic cells and releases their contents into the water treatment system. While most of these substances are harmless, some have been discovered to be potentially harmful to human health over the long term, necessitating improvements in the water treatment process where they are known to occur.

These by-products include a whole range of chemicals that are hard enough to pronounce, let alone imagine. These include trihalomethanes (THMs), haloacetates, haloacetonitriles, haloaldehydes, haloketones and halohydrolyfuranones. The trihalomethanes that are produced in association with chlorine are particularly problematic in that the chemicals produced include chloroform, bromodichloromethane and bromoform, all of which can persist in drinking-water and cause human health problems.

As a result of ongoing public health research, links have been found between these chlorination by-products and reproductive problems in women. A link with bladder and colon cancer has also been discovered. Chlorine, however, is not unique in creating these by-products. Employing bromine instead of chlorine produces yet another set of chemical by-products which may prove to be even more problematic than those created by chlorine. While further research into these effects is continuing, operators of large water treatment plants have been exploring other ways of disinfecting water without having to resort to heavy reliance on chlorine or related chemicals that produce potentially hazardous by-products. Current alternatives to chlorine include chloromine, chlorine dioxide and ozone. Modern processes also include the effective use of non-chemical disinfectants such as ultraviolet light.

Chloromine is a mixture of chlorine and ammonia. Though it is a more complex substance than chlorine, it is less reactive with organic materials such as plant matter and animal and human waste. As a result, it releases fewer disinfection by-products than chlorine. Though chloromine possesses the same residual power as chlorine to continue disinfecting water as it advances into the distribution network, it is a weaker disinfectant than chlorine and thus not suitable for the earliest stage of the treatment process. As it is less reactive and more stable than chlorine, it is more valuable as a disinfection agent that fights against bacterial contamination once treated water has left the plant and begun its way through the distribution network.

Chloromine does, however, have one very pronounced drawback: in higher concentrations it is known to be highly toxic to fish. In addition, it is similar to chlorine in that in higher concentrations it has also been implicated as a human health hazard. It is therefore important to constantly monitor chloromine, both in treatment plants and in the delivery systems that bring treated water to our homes and workplaces.

Chlorine dioxide is something of a wonder chemical. It is as or even more effective than chlorine at killing bacteria, viruses and protozoa. It is also very effective at eliminating parasites that historically have been resistant to chlorine such as *Giardia* and *Cryptosporidium*. Another advantage of chlorine dioxide is that it does not form potentially harmful or carcinogenic disinfection by-products such as trihalomethanes.

The bad news is that chlorine dioxide generates different but perhaps equally problematic by-products of its own, including chlorate and chlorite, which in higher concentrations are known to cause health problems in humans. Another limitation of chlorine dioxide is that because of its chemical composition it cannot be easily transported. As a result, if it is to be used, it must be manufactured on site at the water treatment facility. The cost of this manufacture makes chlorine dioxide far more expensive than simple chlorine.

In order to address the problems associated with the human health effects of chlorine and related chemical disinfectants, high-tech water treatment plants are now employing ozone to neutralize bacteria, viruses and protozoa that make water unsafe to drink. The use of ozone offers a number of advantages over traditional chlorinated disinfectants. Ozone is a powerful antibacterial agent that also works very effectively in removing trace organic materials while improving the appearance, taste and odour of the water. Most importantly, the use of ozone does not result in any chlorinated by-products.

If there is a drawback to the use of ozone, it is that it is expensive. Moreover, its effectiveness is brief compared to the downstream benefits that accrue in the distribution system from the continuing disinfection capacity of chlorine. Water treatment experts have discovered that the most effective way to employ ozone disinfection is in tandem with the addition of low levels of chlorine or chloromine to the water as it enters the distribution stage.

There is one other drawback to the use of ozone. While ozone does not generate chlorinated by-products, its use does produce small concentrations of bromate and formaldehyde. As both of these compounds are only known to cause health problems at high concentrations, the present hazard is very small. There is concern, however, that this could change as water treatment facilities rely more heavily on ozone as a disinfectant. More research is required.

Outbreaks of water-borne disease have driven innovation in the water treatment community. The city of Edmonton experienced a *Giardia* outbreak in 1982 that was linked to 895 cases of illness. That scare prompted a vigorous response, first by the city's water department and later by EPCOR, the city-owned water and power utility.

The response included increased time for chlorine to be in contact with the water; use of activated carbon particles to improve the water's taste, smell and colour; plus the use of electronic monitors on the system's clarifiers and filters. Remote sensing and electronic monitoring of this kind have ushered in a new era of water-quality security. Today, in Edmonton alone, EPCOR performs as many 109,000 tests a year on the region's drinking-water, monitoring 326 different physical, chemical and microbiological parameters. EPCOR also installed what was at the time one of the largest UV treatment systems in the world. In 2002, Edmonton became the first Canadian city of its size to have its drinking-water protected with UV treatment.

Ultraviolet light has long been recognized for its disinfectant qualities. Before it was employed in leading-edge water treatment processes in Europe, it was used in fish hatcheries to disinfect water without harming the fish. Recent research has demonstrated that proper application of ultraviolet light can effectively eliminate bacteria, viruses and protozoans such *Giardia* and *Cryptosporidium* from water. While in common use in water treatment processes in Europe for a decade or more, only the most advanced facilities in Canada are presently employing this technology to improve drinking-water safety.

If there is a drawback to the use of ultraviolet light, it is that its effect is temporary and requires the addition of small amounts of chlorine to ensure residual post-treatment protection as the water enters the distribution system. The combination of ultraviolet light and small concentrations of chlorine, however, has been found to be very effective in producing the highest-quality drinking-water with minimal undesirable by-products.

Tremendous breakthroughs are presently being made in the development of cost-effective membrane filtration in water treatment processes. New systems are being developed that permit the large-scale nano-filtering of water to remove even the tiniest viruses, bacteria and suspended particles as well as *Giardia* and *Cryptosporidium*. Such filtering has the capacity to not only clarify water and improve its taste, but to actually soften it through the removal of metals such as iron and manganese.

Membrane filtration is one of the most exciting advancing domains in the field of water treatment. Further developments in this field could one day revolutionize the way we treat drinking-water in Canada and around the world.

Though most of the current concerns relating to long-term human health implications of water treatment processes revolve around the use of chlorine and other reagents which result in by-products, concern is also being expressed about the use of aluminum and the introduction of high fluorides into drinking-water distribution systems. While there is no current evidence that the use of compounds such as aluminum sulphate to help remove suspended particles from water cause health problems directly, aluminum's link to diseases such as Alzheimer's and Parkinson's is being explored in public-health circles. More research is required to determine whether there is any relation between the use of aluminum in water treatment and the onset of these diseases.

For more than a century, scientists have been able to make a link between fluoride presence in small concentrations in water and improved dental health in humans. While higher concentrations are known to cause discoloration of teeth in children and some bone ailments, the amount of fluoride in Canadian water supplies is strictly regulated to prevent human health hazards.

It is interesting to note that some dental professionals claim to be seeing more cavities in young children who regularly drink bottled water that has not been fluoridated.

≈

Bottled Water:
Many Times More Expensive than Oil

WHILE BOTTLED WATER CAN BE VALUABLE when local water supplies are not safe, Canadians seem to have little understanding of what bottled water costs and where it comes from. Canadians are also confused about the quality of bottled water relative to local tap water.

In a city like Vancouver, Edmonton, Calgary or Toronto, you can fill a 500 mL bottle with tap water 20 times for 1¢. That same bottle of water can cost you $1.50 at a convenience store. Even with valuing the plastic bottle extravagantly at 10¢, that makes the bottled water some 2,800 times more expensive than tap water. In many cases, not only is the water quality the same, it is the same water, only priced 2,800 times higher.

This triumph of marketing over common sense becomes very evident when the price of water is compared to the price of oil:

> 1 barrel = 42 U.S. petroleum gallons
>
> 1 U.S. gallon = 3.78 litres
>
> therefore 1 barrel = 158.76 litres
>
> 158.76 litres will fill 317 500 mL bottles

If you were to fill each of these 317 half-litre bottles with water and sell them for $1.50 each, you would realize $475.50 per barrel, or 7.9 times the value of a barrel of oil (based on an oil price of $60 a barrel).

There are a lot of myths associated with bottled water that, like the myth of limitless abundance of fresh water in Canada, need to be dispelled. Some people think bottled water is safer than municipal tap water, but there is no evidence to support this. Bottled water is often not as perfectly clean as we are led to believe. Like most drinking-water, bottled water has harmless, naturally occurring bacteria. Under the Food and Drugs Act, however, bottled water is required to be free of disease-causing organisms. Nor is bottling necessarily the safest way to store water. A 1988 Health Canada study of bottled water kept at room temperature for 30 days showed a substantial increase in bacterial count. Health Canada recommends that while travelling,

Canadians are advised to avoid bottled water unless it is carbonated or disinfected.

Corporate Knights magazine, in its 2006 special issue on water and pollution, dispelled a number of popular myths about bottled water:

> **Myth:** Bottled water comes from a "pure" source such as a bubbling mountain stream.
>
> > **Fact:** Some 40 per cent of all bottled water comes from a municipal source rather than a natural spring, including Coca-Cola's Dasani and PepsiCo's Aquafina brands.
>
> **Myth:** The plastic bottles from bottled water are reused or recycled.
>
> > **Fact:** About 90 per cent of the bottles from bottled water are thrown out after one use, creating a massive solid waste problem globally. These bottles take 1,000 years to biodegrade.
>
> **Myth:** Bottled water comes from a fairly local source unless otherwise indicated.
>
> > **Fact:** Nearly one quarter of bottled water produced crosses at least one national border to reach consumers. Transportation costs are a large part of its price.
>
> **Myth:** Bottled water is consumed in place of sugary fruit drinks, pop or juice.
>
> > **Fact:** The majority of bottled water is consumed as a substitute for tap water.
>
> **Myth:** Bottled water comes from plentiful sources.
>
> > **Fact:** The Coca-Cola water bottling plant in India has been accused of causing water shortages in 50 surrounding villages.

The $100-billion bottled water industry is a market-based solution to a global water crisis that does little to ameliorate the problems that have caused that crisis. The purchase of bottled water is not likely to improve your local water infrastructure; it does not result in restoration of the region from which you derive your water supply; and, because of transportation costs, it does nothing to reduce greenhouse gas emissions in response to the climate change threat.

≈

Drinking-Water Supply in Canada in the Future

ON THE SURFACE, Canadians should have little to worry about when it comes to water management and supply. Indeed, Canada is endowed with one of the greatest per capita fresh water supplies in the world. Canada also possesses some of the most sophisticated and reliable water treatment technology in the world. This technology is supported by excellent ongoing scientific research and constant refinements in management and operational practices.

If this is the case, then why do real concerns exist in this country regarding our future ability to supply clean drinking-water to our citizens? There is no single answer to this question. The crisis we have created for ourselves with respect to drinking-water supply in Canada resides in a number of important cultural and economic considerations which include how we value water; the current state of our drinking-water infrastructure; the administrative processes by which we manage and maintain our infrastructure assets; and shortcomings in our ability to protect the watersheds that provide our water for treatment.

Put simply, Canadian drinking-water security is being challenged by our attitudes about limitless abundance, aging and inadequate infrastructure, poor asset management and inadequate watershed protection practices. Most Canadians have trouble understanding this because they can afford to take for granted the water that comes out of their taps.

In explaining the problem to Canadians, it is helpful to recognize that, while we have lots of water, it is not always available when and where we want it. Some increasingly populated regions, particularly in western Canada, are semi-arid, meaning they don't receive enough rainfall to grow forests. Water scarcity is becoming an issue on the southern prairies and in other dry areas of Canada, including south-central British Columbia. Climate change is already beginning to aggravate already existing problems related to scarcity in these areas.

In coming to terms with Canada's current drinking-water challenges, it is also important to understand that it costs a great deal of money to design, build and operate reliable water treatment systems. Historically, Canadians in general have not paid the true costs associated with drinking-water supply. As of 2006, for example, only 56 per cent of urban water in Canada was metered. Estimates show that consumption in unmetered areas is almost double: 488 litres per person per day, compared to 288 litres per person in a metered home. As a result Canadians are not forced to consider how much they use and are not generally motivated to practise conservation. Canada cannot, however, afford to continue down this road.

As revenues generated from water users seldom reflect the true cost of supplying that water, municipalities do not always have the revenue they need to operate and maintain water treatment facilities to the necessary standard. This is an issue of asset management. As most revenues from water supply go into general revenue accounts not linked in any way to replacement costs of such facilities, many Canadian communities do not have the capacity to cost-effectively manage the full life cycle of water treatment infrastructure in a way that will allow such facilities to pay for their own operation and for their ultimate replacement when they have reached the end of our their useful life expectancy. Instead, municipalities rely upon federal and provincial grants to upgrade and replace facilities when they are no longer efficient or are too small to meet expanded needs created by population growth and economic development. The problem, however, is that much of Canada's water treatment and delivery infrastructure is almost the same age and is in need of replacement within the same general time frame. What we have done is little different than buying exactly the automobile you want — even if it was very expensive — and then not putting money aside to properly maintain it or replace it once it wears out. A lot of Canadian communities are about to find themselves worrying about wheels.

Inadequate infrastructure is one of the most serious challenges facing our water systems. Across Canada, many municipalities are facing severe infrastructure deficits for both water and waste-water services. The government of Canada recently reported that the nation's wastewater treatment facilities had exhausted 63 per cent of their useful life by 2003.

An Ontario report found that in that province alone, $30- to $40-billion of new investment in water and wastewater facilities was required. In Alberta, at least $290-million was required immediately in 2006, with perhaps a billion more in the coming decades. It has been estimated that some $72-billion will be required to upgrade water delivery systems nationwide. At this time at least, that money does not exist, suggesting that many Canadian communities are going to face greater vulnerability to failure of their water treatment systems in the near future. As the Walkerton Inquiry warned, what happened in that small, pleasant Ontario town could happen almost anywhere in Canada. We need to act to ensure that it doesn't. To do that we may need to reform our system.

The public sector is reacting to growing concerns related to drinking-water security. Across Canada, governments are tightening regulatory requirements and making better efforts to control and monitor water quality. Some programs, such as Alberta's Water for Life strategy, show real promise in increasing public awareness of water issues. But overall, our society is still behaving as if water were an infinite resource. It is not. The myth of limitless abundance of fresh water in Canada has to be dispelled. If we want to be able to rely on water as the foundation of our prosperity in the future, we have to begin to treat it as a valuable resource in its own right.

Our ability to consistently deliver a safe and reliable supply of water depends on at least two key factors: securing a sustainable quantity and quality of raw water; and building and managing sustainable systems for its treatment, distribution and effective demand management. The challenges Canada presently faces in these areas will require that municipal planners and water managers make significant changes to existing water system management strategies to permit them to deliver safe and reliable water to the Canadian public in the future. New tools will have to be adopted to allow communities to meet the challenges they face in dealing with infrastructure issues as they relate to drinking-water security.

The band-aid solutions we are presently employing no longer work. The challenges we are facing can be overcome, but solutions will require broad participation of all sectors of our society. It is no longer enough to allow citizens to sit back and expect water quality and availability problems to be solved for them by proxy solely through technology and infrastructure. It will take the full effort of government, industry and citizenry to create a sustainable drinking-water future in Canada. What Canada effectively needs to begin progress toward sustainability is a new water ethic — and everyone has to be involved in creating and fulfilling this.

Creating a new consciousness of the value of our fresh water resources in Canada will not be easy. Our attitudes and habits with respect to limitless abundance are deeply entrenched in the Canadian psyche and will take time to change. The pathway to such a change, however, is quite clear. At least ten linked approaches have been identified.

1. The need for a new water ethic in Canada

For the nearly 500 years that have passed since Cartier sailed up the St. Lawrence, that most historic of Canadian rivers, water has made us wealthy. As is often the custom with wealthy people, we have, over time, lost touch with the source and true nature of our wealth. Ours is one of the few cultures that have ever had the luxury of being able to take water for granted. But now, in a country that is not even a century and a half old, things have definitely changed. We have discovered to our dismay that the qualities that make water so diversely valuable to us are the same qualities that easily allow it to become contaminated, polluted or lost. As our population has grown and the range of our agricultural, industrial and recreational activities multiplied, we have strained our water resources. At the same time, we have come up against the limits of what we know and can predict about how much water we will have in the future.

Though we cling tenaciously to the image we created of ourselves as a nation of wild rivers and infinitely available, sparkling clean water, we are undone by what we see happening right in front of our very eyes. This is not the only place on the planet, however, where this is happening. Canada is a microcosm of what is happening to water and the world. The largely uninhabited parts of Canada still have plenty of clean, fresh water. At the same time, many inhabited areas of our country will be facing serious water quality and availability issues in the near future and some parts of our country are already in crisis with respect to the availability of water. From this it is easy to determine the direction history is flowing in with respect to this most important of all natural resources. Problems associated with water in Canada are not going to go away. It is time for water to re-enter Canadian consciousness.

Even though passionate advocates for water conservation and aquatic ecosystem restoration can be found in every region of the country, most people still take water completely for granted. The reason for this is simple. We have created an elaborate system that allows Canadians to think that someone else will always take care of water on their behalf. It is as though all of our intelligence and energy is being applied to ensuring that the public doesn't really need to play anything more than a token part in water conservation and stewardship. Water is what comes out of the tap or the bottle. A whole industry exists to make sure Canadians don't have to worry. We have made a business out of solving problems rather than preventing them.

In the real world of everyday water management, it is widely recognized that it is going to be more expensive and more complicated to guarantee reliable sources of high quality water for our society in the future. It is also realized that the scale and capacity of our systems must increase. As an expert water panel in Ontario reported, "systems must join together to better manage risks, increase the depth of their expertise, gain economies of scale and scope and help the highest-cost customers." While innovations in technology and training should reduce water treatment costs, sooner or later technological proxies will not be enough to address the problems we are creating for ourselves. It is only a matter of time before Canadians will have to become as conscious of water conservation and quality protection as the rest of the world.

Understanding of what is happening to our water cannot be confined to professional water management circles. It has to exist also universally at the public level where everyday people must be called upon to consider how much water should flow through the nation's industrial, agricultural and municipal taps. Water is something we all have to understand. The easiest way to reduce the impact of future trends, and buy time for further technological innovation, is to reduce water use and contamination. Unless everyone participates in solutions to water supply and quality issues, however, we will be unable to reform our water ethic and will continue to run the risk of falling into our own infrastructure trap.

We need to build new facilities — lots of them. This presents huge opportunity. The need to build a new water supply system in Canada should be seen as an opportunity not just to create a new national water ethic but to get out of existing infrastructure traps; as an opportunity to create an economic boon to the country based on the development and testing of new technology and systems that will allow us to become a world leader in water management; and as an opportunity to do things better so as to meet the needs of a growing country in a rapidly changing global economic and atmospheric climate.

2. Preventing wholesale waste

We have a large and very elaborate water system in Canada that is not consistently maintained. We waste a staggering amount of water and money through leakage in existing systems. There are many Canadian communities that lose 25 per cent of the water they pay to treat, through leakage from their distribution network. Many justify this by claiming that it would be more expensive to fix the leaks than it is to pay for the treatment of the water that is being lost. What is clearly not being recognized is that when large volumes of water can escape a distribution system, whatever surrounds that system will ultimately find its way into it. Negative pressure in water pipelines can draw pathogens into the system. The leakier the system, the greater the intake of pathogens resulting from low-pressure waves created by starting and stopping supply pumps. Unrepaired leaks can lead to the buildup of pathogenic biofilms on the inside of pipes or, even worse, heavy loads of sudden and unexpected contamination.

Communities with serious leak problems are symbols of what is presently wrong with current asset management philosophy and water distribution system management in much of Canada. Name, if you can, a single private-sector operator that would tolerate the loss of one-quarter of its total production to complete and untraceable dissipation within a supposedly closed distribution system. With proper valuing of water and appropriate long-term asset management there is simply no need for such waste.

The City of Edmonton had similarly high percentages of loss from its system when it contracted with EPCOR to solve the problem. The job took time, but with regular maintenance budgeted into the cost of water over a prolonged period, EPCOR was able to reduce the number of system breaks from 1,500 to 300 and to reduce loss to less than 4.7 per cent each year. As a condition of their contract for supplying Edmonton, EPCOR will now lose money if any more than 4.7 per cent of the city's treated water supply is lost through leaks.

Relatively inexpensive new technology makes it far easier to detect leaks without having to rely on guesswork and expensive exploratory excavation. All it appears to take to solve the leakage problem is a different attitude toward asset and infrastructure management. To turn the tide, it is important to commit to catching up with the problem and to stay on top of the problem once you do catch up with it.

3. Making sure what we already have works

Canada can also do a great deal in support of improvements to its water systems by simply enforcing laws that presently exist. While both federal and provincial governments cite budget cuts and other reasons for their failure in this important domain of mandated public responsibility, there is no excuse for not enforcing our own laws. Governments that fail to do so leave themselves open to be publicly censured for failure of duty and due care.

We need to immediately reform our current regulatory system so that it provides the direction for our society that only laws can provide. There is a great deal of efficiency that can be gained in the management of our country's water system by simply ensuring that water operators have legal incentives to invest in better monitoring, infrastructure improvements and innovative water quality systems. The failure to enforce existing regulations encourages laxness in both operation and planning and penalizes responsible operators and utilities that bear the full costs of operating at or beyond current standards.

Our governments have rarely held operators accountable for failing to meet essential regulatory requirements or for damage done to public health and the environment. In fact, studies show that publicly run operators are among the most frequent offenders. This is because many municipal governments are protected by limitations on liability and have the capacity to pass the costs of non-compliance on to taxpayers. There is also a difficult conflict: since provincial governments often provide capital grants to municipalities for publicly run water facilities, they also understand that strict enforcement could require expensive upgrades. In many cases, governments that carry a regulatory responsibility also understand that by prosecuting offenders they would actually be prosecuting themselves.

Breakdowns or system failures almost always happen in small communities of 1,000 to 4,000 citizens that rely on suspect sources for their water, and where technologically unsophisticated systems are operated by amateurs without adequate oversight. The numbers are significant. In Ontario, for example, 101 sewage facilities were out of compliance with provincial government limits in 2002. These 101 instances of non-compliance were penalized with a total of three charges and one fine — a $10,000 penalty for failing to ensure the facility was run by a licensed operator. This situation occurs in many other jurisdictions as well.

Of the 78 First Nations reserve water operations in Alberta, only 14 were fully certified, as recently as February of 2006. Numbers like this are not only indicative of enforcement shortfalls but also serve to show us that communities are struggling to attract and keep qualified staff.

Owners and operators of water and wastewater systems will invest in their operations if they are held liable for poor performance. The structure for encouraging this kind of investment is in place now. We should be using it.

4. Getting out of our own infrastructure trap

Because our growing population is generating more complex water treatment problems, we should expect the cost of such treatment to rise as more sophisticated processes become necessary to remove problematic new contaminants and by-products from source water. In order to control those costs, innovative new technology will need to be employed in the development of larger integrated systems. This will demand that governments at all levels challenge existing water delivery models.

One of the most serious traps we have created for ourselves relates to current infrastructure grant arrangements in Canada. Many municipalities do not create freestanding utilities funded by customers, because current infrastructure programs do not demand that such facilities be managed with the future cost of replacement budgeted into the current cost of operation. They can do this because they know they won't have to recover the full costs of operating and replacing this infrastructure. Instead, they can go to the federal and provincial governments for grants whenever they need them. This allows municipalities to drain their water utilities of resources during periods of budget cutting, permitting maintenance and operation to suffer while putting the public at risk.

The Ontario Water Works Association and the Ontario Municipal Water Association are among many industry groups that believe such subsidies or grants are unproductive. They believe that in most cases such grants "reward those who neglect their infrastructure and punish those who are proactive and operate efficiently and effectively."

Success in addressing future needs and circumstances will require that governments at all levels challenge existing service delivery models. This process will likely require a more progressive attitude toward valuing water and toward public and private-sector partnerships.

5. The valuing and realistic pricing of water supply

Some of the circumstances our emerging water supply situation is creating will demand a sharp and unpopular deviation from the status quo in terms of the way we value water. Beyond affordable supply at the level of basic needs it becomes necessary to pay the full cost of water and water delivery so that we can invest in necessary system improvements and new infrastructure.

A key starting point is coming to grips with the real cost of water. Water is not a free good — it is a precious resource that should be used responsibly and conserved. According to the Organization for Economic Cooperation and Development, Canadians pay some of the lowest water rates in the world. The advantages of ascribing a value to water and charging users at rates related to this value have been explored in many water-scarce countries around the world. These advantages include the provision of funds for ongoing water developments; reduction of demands on the public sector for the capital and recurrent costs associated with providing water; the release of water for high-value use; assistance in prioritization of water allocation; and the resolution of conflicts between user groups. Advantages also include the provision of water through demand management for environmental services and aquatic ecosystem health and the reduction of water use through demand management.

Governments in Canada see a great number of political obstacles to introducing water pricing policies. The main obstacle appears to be the potential for short-term unpopularity that will cost votes for governments in power. The second major obstacle is the fear that increased prices for water could create inflation, especially in those regions where water plays a central role in the economy. Around the world, however, most examples point to the benefits of appropriate water pricing outweighing the short-term political disadvantages.

In many Canadian communities, water rates remain low because they are subsidized by municipal governments through allocations to water utilities in municipal budgets. A recent report by an expert panel reviewing Ontario's water system noted that municipalities in the province recovered only 65 per cent of the total costs of providing water services.

While low rates may create the illusion of affordability, they limit opportunities for reinvestment and prevent overall system sustainability. Reflecting on the capital-intensive nature of water and wastewater services, the report noted that "utilities are starved for the funds they need to maintain their systems properly." Ultimately, rates that do not reflect the full cost of producing and delivering the service eventually lead to a gap between what the system is *expected* to deliver and what it *can* deliver without continual subsidies.

Provincial governments in Canada use water licence systems to control how much water is withdrawn, for what purpose, and by whom. But there are many instances where the true cost of treating and distributing water is hidden by subsidies or absorbed by the tax system.

In order for Canada to afford the infrastructure improvements it needs, customers of water and wastewater services will ultimately have to fund the full cost of building, operating and maintaining the system. Proponents of this notion cite two reasons. First, it creates a pool of funding that is sufficient for the continuing maintenance of the system — as long as the contributions remain dedicated to the system and are not diverted to other uses. Second, it sends an appropriate price signal — one that reminds us to conserve and make more prudent use of our resources. If water is free, we assign it no value. If it has no value, we waste it without thought.

The argument has been put forward that if governments were to mandate that Canadian pricing regimes move toward full-cost recovery, then our public and private water utilities would be able to properly maintain existing facilities and build new ones, and together we would succeed in conserving our water resource.

Politicians, of course, argue that no one wants to pay more for basic services. Many Canadians also consider water a free good or a right, on principle. Most also recognize that since customers are used to paying rates well below the real cost of water, the transition will require both time and continuous public education.

6. Exploring public/private partnerships

While this remains a controversial issue in some areas of Canada, there is no question that private-sector organizations can sometimes offer resources to communities that the public sector may not otherwise be able to effectively provide. All levels of government and private-sector partners need to work together to deliver effective watershed management strategies, create value through facility sharing, and seek the benefits of alternative service-delivery methods.

Partnerships between governments and private-sector actors allow the public sector to share costs and risk while maintaining a public interest in a key, vital service to local communities. This does not mean governments should necessarily divest themselves of assets and retreat to a purely regulatory role. Rather, using their interest or ownership in water system assets, governments can ensure that predetermined levels of service are maintained and costs controlled without playing a direct management and operational role.

In certain circumstances, public/private partnerships can offer a number of potential benefits. First, in a well-structured partnership the risks of cost overruns, service demand and schedule delays are borne by the private sector, not the taxpayer. Competitive tendering can encourage innovative private-sector solutions to facility management, design and construction.

These partnerships also offer government greater flexibility to tailor projects to best meet local needs.

Opponents of public/private partnerships often object that these projects experience higher costs, since the private sector must borrow at higher interest rates than governments can because government is considered a less risky investment — governments can always return to the taxpayer in the event of cost overruns. Yet, despite higher borrowing costs, the evidence points to the contrary. In the United Kingdom, reports by the Treasury Department indicate that public/private partnerships experience overall cost savings of 20 per cent compared to publicly procured operations. The report also found that only 24 per cent of these projects were delivered late, compared to 70 per cent in the public sector. Cost overruns occurred only 22 per cent of the time under these partnerships, compared to 73 per cent in the public sector.

Because of the cost and scale of what is required for overcoming current infrastructure inadequacies, partnerships between governments and the private sector will become more important and more common. Contractual arrangements between public systems and private-sector partners will also become more sophisticated to ensure that failures in these arrangements in the past are not repeated.

7. Source protection

As has been proven by New York City and Vancouver, one of the most cost-effective and efficient mechanisms for reliably supplying clean drinking-water to large populations is through the protection of upland watersheds. Source protection saves a great deal of expense by ensuring that the water to be treated is already at a high standard of quality before it even enters the treatment and distribution system.

There is a maxim in water management that suggests that what we do on the land inevitably shows up in the water. If you allow industry to operate in the area from which you draw your drinking-water, expect to have to deal with industrial by-products in your water treatment plant. If there is extensive agriculture upstream, expect to have to manage agricultural chemicals and nutrients. A key element of source protection is the prevention of inappropriate development in that part of the watershed that supplies drinking-water. Where this is not possible, careful regulation of land use may be necessary to prevent poor initial water quality from affecting the cost of water treatment and infrastructure maintenance.

8. Integrated watershed management

Our need for reliable water supplies; our resulting tradition of relying on dams, reservoirs and large-scale infrastructure for water storage; and our reliance on rules of good engineering practice and regulatory regimes are mutually dependent and tend to stabilize and affirm one another to create the notion that what we are doing now is the preferred way of managing our water resources. This long-held notion, however, stands in the way of emerging new ideas of how to manage water in a more integrated way.

We are used to having important decisions about water management made as zero-sum calculations undertaken in closed decision loops. Our water management habits favour controllable, predictable, technologically advanced systems that function reliably within established risk thresholds and a rigidly fixed regulatory environment. We are so used to this form of management that we have difficulty accepting that more adaptive ways of managing may be necessary in emerging circumstances in which different approaches may be required to get more out of limited supplies of water or in scenarios in which risk cannot be controlled as effectively as it was in the past. Both of these situations are beginning to appear in western Canada, where some areas are becoming genuinely water scarce and whole regions are experiencing changing precipitation and water availability regimes.

It may no longer be adequate in certain cases to rely on consultation processes in which different stakeholder groups and the public at large are invited to offer their opinion on management plans or scenarios that have already been developed by experts. These processes may have to be replaced by expanded processes in which all bona fide interests participate in co-generation of knowledge, co-design of solutions and co-decision-making that involves taking shared responsibility for water management outcomes.

At present, responsibility for management of water resources is atomized among too many jurisdictions that often put their own interests ahead of the overall health of the watershed. The new Canadian movement toward the creation of watershed basin councils, authorities and trusts should be vigorously encouraged. Support, however, must go beyond token recognition of the need for citizen involvement in new ways of managing watersheds on an integrated basis. In order to prevent frustration and burnout, support must include adequate funding for research, programming and continuous collaboration. Moreover, if integrated watershed management is to be truly achieved, governments will have to download more than just responsibility for water quality and availability to basin councils. They will ultimately have to ensure that such groups also have the *authority* to make changes in the way their basins are managed.

9. Recognizing future challenges and threats

Canadians have to face the realization that water supply in many areas of the country is limited. Serious and continuous conservation will be necessary, not just to reduce real costs associated with treatment and distribution infrastructure but also to ensure that everyone has enough water as populations grow and climate change affects existing precipitation patterns and timing in many parts of the West.

The current climate of our planet is maintained through radiation balance of solar heating and infrared cooling, moderated through the effects of clouds and trace gases; and the present temperatures at the surface of the Earth where we live are sustained through the action of a greenhouse effect. There is now a scientific consensus that increases of trace gases, including carbon dioxide, have already increased the mean temperature of the Earth's system of land, oceans and ice. Moreover, this warming is expected to accelerate, not only because of the accumulation of carbon dioxide, but also because of positive feedback from changes that have already occurred. Most serious of all, relatively small changes in average temperature are capable of causing enormous changes to the physical mechanisms that maintain the heat and water balance of the Earth.

The critical problems of water resources in the Canadian West have been identified in several seminal studies over the past decade. Climate impacts on this region may, at the very least, include a small increase in the average temperature, which may cause relatively large changes in runoff by increasing the frequency of melt events, even without additional increases in precipitation. The sensitivity of water storage in snowpack and glaciers to increased temperatures will be greater in the south and at lower elevations, where the mean temperature is closer to the freezing point. The effect of warmer temperatures will also shift the timing of the runoff freshet to earlier in the spring, thus depleting the storage capability that would have been available for the later summer season. The consequences of these changes in water storage capacity and timing of the runoff will have consequences for the competing demands on water resources, which are expected to become greater in the coming decades. This poses a serious challenge to water managers and users.

We will need to recognize always the complexity of this issue and the crucial importance of keeping up with science and with unfolding events related to understanding of climate and other impacts on water, especially in the Canadian West.

10. A commitment to educating the public

In order to facilitate the changes in our management of water and justify the cost of improvements to our country's drinking-water delivery systems, the public needs to know a great deal more about how their drinking-water happens. We are heading in some important new directions with respect to the management and operation of drinking-water supply and distribution systems. These directions include changes in governance; full cost recovery; more comprehensive record-keeping; scheduled-maintenance accountability; and mandatory improvements in long-term asset management. These changes will cause some municipalities to reconsider the mechanisms by which they operate, now and in the future.

Canadians are also facing an infrastructure replacement crisis that will be difficult and very expensive to address. For this reason we can expect a greater number of system failures that are not going to be perceived in an appropriate light unless the public has a better understanding of the state of our systems and what needs to be done to improve them. Unless the public is invited into the debate, there will continue to be unproductive resistance to badly needed policy changes, and unnecessary delays in acting upon the need to upgrade a large part of our national drinking-water infrastructure. It will be difficult to get the billions of dollars needed for infrastructure improvement if the voting public doesn't know what is needed and why. Canadians will keep taking clean drinking-water for granted or — even more problematic — they will simply cave in to market persuasion and rely more and more on bottled water, which will create a different set of problems.

We are at a crossroads with water management in Canada. Canadians remain among the world's highest per capita water users. Only by persistently and effectively reaching out to the public can we dispel the myth of limitless abundance of clean, fresh water. Only by educating the public can we instill a conservation ethic that will ensure that water availability and quality issues do not limit our social and economic future.

Three: What We Can Learn from Others

The Rosenberg Forum

IN WESTERN CANADA, governments like to go it alone. They generally distrust outsiders who propose different ways of thinking about managing water, preferring homegrown solutions to the problems they face. But as our populations and economies grow, we will need to learn from others who have been in situations similar to ours earlier in their own national development. The Rosenberg Forum is one of many vehicles Canadians use to learn how others deal with problems similar to ours.

The Rosenberg International Forum on Water Policy was created in 1996. It is named for Richard Rosenberg, a former chairman of the Bank of America. Upon Mr. Rosenberg's retirement in 1994, the bank endowed the University of California in his name with resources to help support a biennial invitational water forum for the world's leading water scholars and senior water management practitioners. The main thrust of these forums is the resolution of conflict emerging from transboundary water issues. The first four of these meetings were held in San Francisco, U.S.A.; Barcelona, Spain; Canberra, Australia; and Ankara, Turkey.

The Fifth Biennial Rosenberg International Forum on Water Policy took place in Banff, Alberta, from September 6 to 11, 2006. Participants included 52 scholars and water managers from 24 countries. The theme was "Upland Watershed Management in an Era of Global Climate Change." The event included a two-day pre-forum field trip through the UNESCO Canadian Rockies World Heritage Site to examine modern upland watershed practices; two days of formal presentations; and a post-forum field trip to the Columbia River Basin, which had been the subject of a case study at Rosenberg Forum IV, held in Ankara in 2004. It was on the post-forum field trip that participants visited Takakkaw Falls in Yoho National Park.

The keynote address at the Rosenberg is usually given by a head of state. In Turkey, it was offered by Suleyman Demirel, a former president of Turkey and the architect of the Peace Pipeline concept in the Middle East. In Canada the keynote address was offered by Don Lowry, the president and CEO of EPCOR, an Edmonton-based water and electricity utility.

Mr. Lowry was the first private-sector person to be invited to give the keynote opening address. What the forum saw as vitally important about his presentation is that he clearly underscored the need for a new water ethic in Canada; the need to get out of current infrastructure traps; the importance of valuing and realistically pricing water; the value and place of private/public partnerships; the urgency of securing sustainable water supplies in Canada and abroad; and the importance of recognizing future challenges and threats such as climate change.

The keynote remarks were followed by formal presentations which included three general sessions on topics related to upland watershed management practices around the world and the implications of global climate change for upland watershed management. These sessions were followed by four case studies which included the Jordan, Saskatchewan and Rhône River Basins and the International Joint Commission, a bilateral institution created a century ago to resolve boundary water disputes between Canada and the United States. These proceedings put into relief that enormous amount that Canada has to learn to keep up with the management of water, especially in the increasingly water-scarce West.

Canada in the Context of Global Change

IN THEIR PAPER "The Emerging Global Water Crisis: Managing Scarcity and Conflict between Water Users," William Jury and Henry Vaux make the claim that the next hundred years will be very different from the century that has just passed in that 3 billion more people are likely to join the 6.5 billion who presently inhabit our planet. The authors argue there are four trends which, if continued, could combine to trigger a global catastrophe in the 21st century. The first is that of steady population growth. The second is the continuing fragmentation and degradation of terrestrial, aquatic and marine ecosystems. Third is climate change, which is already affecting the planet but whose specifics remain uncertain. The fourth and final trend is the depletion of the world's water resources through misuse, overuse and the degradation of water quality.

Jury and Vaux go on to point out that without immediate action and global cooperation, a water supply and water pollution crisis of unimaginable dimensions will confront humanity, limiting food production, access to drinking-water, and the survival of innumerable other life forms. Jury and Vaux base their dire forecast on extrapolation from current human activities and trends on this planet. They identify a number of further trends in this area.

First, unlike estimates of the global supply of scarce minerals or buried hydrocarbons which remain uncertain, planetary supplies of water have been well characterized. There are no large groundwater deposits awaiting human discovery in readily accessible locations. Any new sources that happen to be discovered will be very expensive to develop.

Second, many vital human activities are dependent on groundwater supplies that are being exhausted or contaminated.

Third, much of the population growth of the next century is likely to occur in areas of greatest water shortage. There are no plans for addressing the problems that will inevitably follow. It should be pointed out that not all of these places are in Africa or the high interiors of South America. Many participants at the Rosenberg Forum that took place in Alberta were surprised to find themselves in an area of growing scarcity in which population growth is rapid and unchecked and where limits to water availability are already apparent.

Finally, global economic forces are luring water and land away from food production and toward more lucrative activities, while at the same time encouraging pollution that impairs drinking-water quality for a large and ever-growing segment of the population.

Jury and Vaux also offer some important statistics that place the Canadian situation in a global context. Total global surface runoff has been estimated at about 42,700 cubic kilometres, but because considerably less than this volume is geographically available to us, only about 12,500 km^3 is potentially available for human use. In 1990, it was estimated that about 18 per cent of all available water was being used by humans and that an additional 34 per cent was necessary for ecosystem function. These two needs, however, are projected to require 70 per cent of the available runoff by 2025. Although projected human use is still less than 25 per cent of the surface water supply, humans cannot utilize all of the available surface water without destroying ecosystems that depend on water for survival.

Jury and Vaux go on to report that, based on projections by Malin Falkenmark of the Stockholm International Water Institute and Johan Rockström of the Stockholm Environment Institute, some 29 nations will be classified as water scarce by 2025. Among them will be countries that we would not have expected to have water availability problems, such as the United Kingdom. Of these 29 nations, 17 are predicted to be desperately water scarce. Another 47 nations are expected to be classified as water scarce or water stressed at the same time. Secure sustainable water resources for generations to come in some of these countries will not be possible without population decline or massive — and very expensive — water transfers.

The lesson here is that Canada is not immune to what is happening in the rest of the world. Though they have largely occupied themselves elsewhere, there is no reason the Four Horsemen can't ride the Canadian range. Alberta's population is growing. Terrestrial ecosystem fragmentation and degradation are happening here — and so is climate change. Water availability is already a real concern. Canadians, especially those living in the West, should be mindful of their history. Decade-long droughts have occurred here in the past. In order to secure sustainable water resources for generations to come, urbanites distanced from these realities would be wise to remember this.

Issues of Equity in Canada

SECURING SUSTAINABLE WATER RESOURCES for generations to come is a global issue. We have a great number of problems with water supply in many areas. At present 1.1 billion people on this planet are without reliable sources of drinking-water and 2.6 billion do not have access to adequate sanitation services.

The United Nations has declared reliable access to clean drinking-water a basic human right. This basic human right does not presently appear to extend to all First Nations in Canada. Despite federal oversight, drinking-water quality remains unreliable on federal lands designated as First Nations reserves. In 2005, contaminated water forced the residents of a largely aboriginal community in Kashechewan, Ontario, to evacuate their homes because of water contamination. In the first eight months of 2006, 83 boil water advisories were issued on Indian reserves across Canada. As of this writing, 59 per cent of reserve drinking-water systems were considered to be "at risk."

But it is not just on First Nations reserves that water quality is not an established right. In legal fact this right may not extend to any Canadian. The weakness in public policy in Canada is underscored by University of British Columbia law professor David Boyd in his book *Unnatural Law: Rethinking Canadian Environmental Law and Policy*:

> Many Canadians believe, incorrectly, that they have a right to clean, safe water. While this right may exist at a philosophical level, it does not exist under Canadian law. There is no such right provided in Canada's Constitution, the Charter of Rights and Freedoms, or in the common law. A British Columbia Supreme Court Justice recently ruled in a lawsuit where citizens sought unsuccessfully to halt logging activities in their watershed: "There is not before me an established case for the concept of a 'right' to clean water."

While the ruling that Boyd describes had as much to do with the specific circumstances of the legal case as it did with the right Canadians might claim to clean, safe water, Boyd's point cannot be ignored. While a right to clean water may be part of the contract we assume exists between ourselves and the society in which we live, there are legal circumstances in which that right may not be upheld. That such legal confusion exists in a First World country with abundant water resources could be seen as a national embarrassment. If nothing else it puts into relief gaps in public policy and accountability related to federal versus provincial responsibility for water resources. Whether they are legally entitled or not, part of the Canadian population is assured of high-quality water supply while another part is not.

Canadians should be reminded that issues of equity are important and that aboriginal legal claims related to water rights have been upheld in courts elsewhere, with significant consequences for water policy. In the United States, for example, untested federal treaty conditions relating to water rights have been described as an unknown with almost "thermonuclear" potential to change the water policy landscape, particularly in the water-scarce West. It was clear from the presentations at the Rosenberg Forum that First Nations water rights in parts of Canada have yet to be fully characterized. One wonders what would happen in Canada if all the First Nations in Alberta and Saskatchewan were to suddenly declare that they had had enough of unreliable and unsafe drinking-water supply and sued both the federal and provincial governments over their inability to protect water quality.

This discussion led to the unresolved matter of how much water First Nations may be entitled to under their treaty rights. It has been pointed out that it has been held in some cases in the United States that First Nations are legally entitled to water supplies sufficient to meet the development needs identified in the treaties they signed, even if those water resources have in the meantime been claimed by others. Where these rights are claimed, they predate licences granted later in time. Widespread claiming of these rights could potentially deconstruct the current "first-in-time, first-in-right" water rights hierarchy in parts of the West. Given the antiquated nature of the water rights system based on prior appropriation in Western Canada, such a development south of the border could prove to be both a challenge and an opportunity.

Upland Watershed Protection

CANADIANS ARE TO BE CONGRATULATED on the enlightened manner in which much of the upland mountain headwater region of the Rocky Mountains has been protected as both national and provincial parks. A large portion of the upland region is in almost pristine condition and as such produces a wealth of ecological services that would be expensive if not impossible to provide through engineering infrastructure. Caution is advised, however, with respect to the management of fragile mountain stream ecosystems. While terrestrial ecosystems in the mountain national and provincial parks are well managed, aquatic ecosystems appear to receive less attention.

David Schindler has pointed out that 41 per cent of the flow of the Bow River within Banff National Park was regulated. This regulation is a consequence of the construction of a dam on Lake Minnewanka, which was approved, against considerable opposition to the presence of such structures in national parks, under authorization by an Order in Council under the War Measures Act in 1941. The usual problems associated with dams, however, have manifested themselves, just as opponents predicted. Flow regimes in the Cascade River were dramatically reduced. As no fish ladders were installed back up Cascade Creek, the natural ecosystem declined dramatically. As a result of drawdowns in the winter and refilling in summer, changes in the lake's littoral zone have been dramatic. Since the dam was constructed, lake-bottom fauna changed from 50 per cent macro-invertebrates to over 90 per cent chironomids. Stocking with invasive fish species and diversion of the river around the original channel have virtually destroyed the riparian habitat of the Cascade River.

Upland watershed protection will become more and more important as population growth, diminishment of water supply and climate change conspire to change the hydrology of the Canadian West. While the water storage capacity of the reservoir may be of some importance, the Minnewanka dam is no longer a critical regional source of hydro-electricity. While restoration of the system may be expensive, it should be seen as an option leading up to the expiry of the dam's operating licence in 2032.

Given that water scarcity has already been identified as a potentially limiting factor in the economic and social development of southern Alberta, it may be important to reassess the value of upland areas in the context of water supply and the ecological services they provide. It may be wise to consider special upland designation for no other reason than watershed protection. In examining upland watershed protection options, it should be noted that while our mountain national parks are now considered valuable tourism resources, their original purpose resided as much in water resource protection as in tourism promotion. This was particularly true of large parks like Jasper, which was initially set aside as a forest park in 1907.

As the Oldman River Basin has already been identified as a water-scarce region in which over-allocation could potentially lead to conflict over water use, its upper reaches may be a good candidate for special watershed protection. The proposed 1,400-square-kilometre Andy Russell-I'tai sah kop Park at the headwaters of the Oldman has the highest recorded annual precipitation and snowfall along the eastern slopes of the Rockies in Alberta. While the proposed park would cover less than 4 per cent of the area of the Oldman Basin, it annually generates some 20 per cent to 30 per cent of the river's annual flow. Within this small area are 26 headwater streams and rivers which feed the Castle, Oldman and Waterton systems. Not surprisingly, it is also an area of great natural beauty. One of the lessons of the Rosenberg Forum was that protecting such valuable upland regions will pay for itself over and over again in the value of the ecological services it provides alone.

≈

Irrigation Efficiency

GLOBAL WATER AVAILABILITY is inextricably linked to food production. Without the one, you don't get the other. Bill Jury and Henry Vaux have pointed out that in 1995, about 3,800 cubic kilometres of fresh water was withdrawn from surface and groundwater supplies globally. Of that amount some 2,100 km^3 was consumed, and thus removed from the supply base. Industry and municipal withdrawals are significant, but much of those withdrawals are returned to the supply base, leaving only 6.4 per cent that is actually consumed. Agriculture is by far the dominant global consumer of water, accounting for nearly 85 per cent of all water use. It is projected that we will need to increase food production by nearly 50 per cent in the next 50 years to maintain our present per capita supply. This, of course, assumes that the present productivity of existing farmland does not decline.

Jury and Vaux also point out that despite earlier successes associated with what has widely been called "the Green Revolution," the ratio of global grain stocks to annual consumption has fallen steadily during the last decade. Optimists in the field of global food supply argue that there are many factors that suggest we have little at present to worry about in terms of food production. Crop yields in numerous poor countries are far below maximum attainable yields that have been reached in other regions.

Substantial land is available for agricultural expansion, and the introduction of evolving irrigation technology is sure to increase production far beyond what has historically been possible in areas of marginal rainfall. Optimists also argue that genetic alteration of plant species could greatly improve the productivity of almost all sectors of agriculture.

Jury and Vaux also put forward the contrary case. Pessimists about the great hope of the Green Revolution cite challenges that appear insurmountable. A significant part of the world's agricultural land is being managed unsustainably — including land in Canada — and cannot continue to be farmed indefinitely. Market forces in developing countries are driving the conversion of farmland to urban and industrial use. Loss of topsoil from water and wind erosion is decreasing the fertility of soils all over the world. The most compelling of all arguments offered by pessimists, however, has to do with global water availability. In the next 50 years, we may — quite simply — run out of water.

It is anticipated that irrigation water withdrawals will expand by 685 km³ per year between 1995 and 2025. While water used for this purpose will reduce the per capita water requirement to produce food for a growing population, we will not be able to meet future food production needs unless irrigation methods become more efficient.

Experts in the field have estimated that in 1990, average irrigation efficiency for 118 countries in the world was 43 per cent. In North America this measure is about 53 per cent. (Average irrigation efficiency is here defined as the amount of water required for maximum crop yield divided by the quantity of irrigation withdrawals.) Experts point out that if irrigation efficiency were to be increased by 70 per cent, the need for additional water supply for all sectors could be reduced by 50 per cent by 2025. The total savings would be 944 km³ a year. Such a saving would clearly go a long way to ensure sustainable water resources for generations to come.

Irrigated agriculture produces approximately 40 per cent of the world's food on only 17 per cent of the total land under production. That makes it about 325 per cent more productive than rain-fed agriculture. Irrigation farmers, especially in southern Alberta, are very proud of such statistics, but these numbers are not cause for abandoning efforts to improve the efficiency and productivity of irrigated agriculture. Indeed, efforts to secure sustainable water resources for generations to come will require improvements in the productivity and efficiency of both irrigated and rain-fed agriculture.

Irrigation efficiency of 70 per cent is not impossible in Canada. There are at least four categories of improvement that can be made to enhance the productivity of irrigation farming. They are technical, agronomic, managerial and institutional. Technical improvements entail the utilization of techniques that permit water to be applied uniformly and reduce the losses to evaporation, runoff and deep percolation. Agronomic improvements consist of better agricultural practices that minimize water loss from evaporation. Managerial improvements include improvements in irrigation scheduling and water delivery timing as well as the movement toward demand-based irrigation. Institutional improvements include the development of effective water-user organizations, reducing or eliminating subsidies for irrigation water, and implementing effective conservation incentives. Improvements in rain-fed agricultural productivity are also possible through better methods of rainwater capture, supplemental irrigation and integrated land and soil management.

All of these tools will be necessary to improve the efficiency of agricultural water use. Such improvements will be crucial if Canada wants to both improve agricultural productivity while at the same time allow further population and industrial growth in already water-scarce areas.

≈

Resolving Transboundary Disputes

ESTABLISHED DIVISIONS OF ACCOUNTABILITY for water management between the federal and provincial governments are not adequate to some circumstances. Since Confederation the federal government has deferred to the provinces in domestic and transboundary water issues. While this deference has respected the terms and conditions of the form of cooperative federalism that is at the heart of the Canadian Constitution, there are some situations in which greater federal presence in the handling of transboundary water issues is likely necessary in order to ensure enduring solutions that result in optimal management of our shared resources.

There are two levels at which a stronger federal presence may be useful. The first is in the resolution of transboundary disputes between provinces; the second lies in the domain of transboundary disputes between individual provinces and our u.s. neighbours.

In the case of interprovincial water disputes, the capacity of a given provincial government to respond to basin-wide needs may be limited by jurisdictional self-interest. Similarly, the legal powers of a province may not be adequate to the challenges posed by increasingly complex legislation protecting one country from impacts originating in another. Resolution of such issues may require nation to nation negotiation and cooperation. But, before it can be effective in resolving issues at either of these levels, the federal government in Canada has to come to terms with the absence of a coherent national water policy.

With respect to our relationship with our southern neighbours, a great deal has been written about the very peaceable manner in which our two countries have been able to resolve transboundary water disputes. The relationship between Canada and the United States has been defined for almost a century by the Boundary Waters Treaty, which was signed between the two countries in 1909. This treaty addresses a broad range of transboundary water issues including definition of boundary and transboundary surface waters and the joint study of these waters with reference to their potential use. The treaty establishes mechanisms for the approval of certain uses and permission for obstruction or diversion of transboundary waters that may affect flow volumes in either country. The treaty also contains provisions that prohibit pollution that may result in injury to health or property on either side of the international boundary. The treaty is widely considered as an exemplary model of an international transboundary agreement. In a paper entitled *Thirsty Neighbours: A Century of Canada-US Transboundary Water Governance*, water policy scholar Ralph Pentland and former ijc Commissioner Adèle Hurley wrote that there are many Canadian water policy experts who doubt Canada could negotiate as favourable an agreement as the Boundary Waters Treaty in today's political climate.

Beyond establishing rules for transboundary water management, the Boundary Waters Treaty also created a means for resolving disputes, in the form of the International Joint Commission. The IJC performs two essential functions. It approves remedial or protective works, obstructions or dams on trans-boundary waters, and sets conditions for the operation of such works. It also investigates and makes recommendations on questions relating to operating rules or disputes that are referred to it by either or both governments. The key point here is that the IJC has to be *invited* by one or both federal governments to investigate disputes and collaborate with conflicting parties in the interest of creating durable solutions to transboundary water issues.

While the IJC has enjoyed legendary success in the resolution of such issues, concerns have been growing over its current effectiveness. There is no single reason for this. The biggest reason for the decline in effectiveness of the IJC, however, may reside in the fact that neither Canadian nor U.S. governments are supporting it — or utilizing it — to the extent they once did.

The main issue here is that the powers under the Boundary Waters Treaty are no longer being employed in the manner in which they were in the past. Important transboundary water issues are not being referred to the International Joint Commission to be resolved. Instead of relying on historically successful institutional approaches to dispute resolution, the federal governments in both Canada and the United States are choosing to address these issues in the political domain instead. Pentland and Hurley state it simply: "The International Joint Commission can only be as successful as American and Canadian governments want it to be." When one or both federal governments are disinclined to cooperate on transboundary water issues, the IJC is sidelined. Presently, unilateral actions by individual states and provinces are undermining the spirit and intent of the Boundary Waters Treaty and neutralizing the effectiveness of the IJC. The cases in which the IJC has not been invited to be involved, such as the Devil's Lake issue and pollution on the Columbia River, are highly instructive, for they demonstrate just how quickly the good will created through generations of cooperation can be lost.

Work should be done immediately both on clarifying federal/provincial relations in Canada and on improving relations with the United States with respect to transboundary issues. It is only a matter of time before the most important compacts that exist between the provinces and the treaties Canada has with the U.S.

are no longer adequate to the circumstances we have created on this continent since these treaties were signed.

The Alberta Water for Life Strategy for Sustainability

THE PRESENTATIONS at the Rosenberg Forum on International Water Policy put into relief efforts that are being made worldwide to develop broader collaborations to achieve better water management. At this time, no nation has been able to break through tradition and habit to create a fully adaptive and integrated form of water stewardship that combines water management with land policy in a way that will assure true sustainability.

Everywhere in the world, water managers are working backward from faulty assumptions that form the foundation of contemporary water policy and trying to engineer their way out of the problems they have created for themselves. While this approach leaves the engineering field clearly in charge, it gives society little assurance that our growing challenges related to sustainability will be met and, if in fact they are met, offers no guarantee that the solutions will be equitably available. We get what the marketplace decrees we need. We get saleable technologies and best practices, but we don't always get real solutions. It is up to government to sell real solutions such as population control and environmental restraint, but that is not what the marketplace wants. With unbridled growth one branch of engineering inevitability functions to create new problems that only another branch of engineering can solve. While this perpetual-motion machine powers our economy, it makes it impossible to keep up with the sheer number of difficulties and vulnerabilities we are creating for ourselves. We end up with ever more sophisticated engineering and an ever more diminished world. This downward spiral characterizes water policy and management practice globally in the early 21st century. Unfortunately, it also characterizes our management of the larger global life support system. But not all of our global water issues are related to our excessive reliance on engineering.

Many countries cannot manage water effectively because of historical precedents that cannot be easily escaped. Despite serious efforts, it is almost impossible for a country like Jordan to fulfill the promise of integrated watershed management in the midst of intense regional conflict and uncertainty. While a solid foundation has been laid down for adaptive management in the Rhône River Basin, sheer population size and investment in already existing infrastructure will make wholesale change in water management processes slow if not ultimately impossible.

In Canada, however, no such obstacles exist to the creation of an integrated watershed approach. The country and the provinces are stable politically and economically. Our population is still relatively small and there is still a great deal of slack that can be taken up in the management of our water resources. Though habits of entitlement will be hard to break, a strong case for new strategies for coming together over issues of allocation and use is already being made through such initiatives as the Alberta government's Water for Life strategy.

This strategy recognizes that Alberta is facing significant pressures on its water resources. The strategy accepts that population growth, droughts and agricultural and industrial development are increasing demand on Alberta's water supplies and thus increasing the risk to the health, well-being and economic future of the people who live in the province. The strategy boldly announces that all Albertans have to recognize there are limits to the available water supply and that the province's water resources must be managed within the capacity of individual watersheds. It further recognizes that management of water resources isn't just the responsibility of government. Citizens, communities and industry also must share this responsibility and work together to improve conditions in local watersheds. The strategy also puts Albertans on notice that while the "first-in-time, first-in-right" principle for granting and administering water allocations will be preserved, water allocations will have to become transferable to ensure that society's demands and needs can be met. For the first time, the strategy makes the goal of preserving healthy aquatic ecosystems as important as providing a safe, secure drinking-water supply and reliable, quality supplies of water for sustained economic development.

While not as yet fully funded or implemented, Alberta's Water for Life initiative has the potential to succeed in areas in which other similar approaches have failed. The strategy announces that while earlier domestic water management policies were adequate for the pioneering circumstances confronted by settlers in the newly opened Canadian West, they no longer suffice in a suddenly heavily populated region that faces limits to its social and economic future unless it finds ways to make regional water resources do more and go further than they have in the past.

In June of 2006, a panel of acknowledged world experts on water policy related to both surface and groundwater resources convened in Calgary to examine and review progress toward the provincial government's Water for Life strategy and its Groundwater Action Plan. The proceedings of this Rosenberg sub-forum suggest that the Alberta Water for Life strategy could become a model for others in western Canada who want to break out of long-standing but no longer appropriate habits of water resource management. For it to be successful, however, a number of conditions have to be met.

It is important that in the face of accelerated energy production and population growth all efforts be made to advance the research and regulatory activities needed to protect water resources that could be threatened. This is particularly true in the case of coalbed methane extraction and oilsands development.

It is also important that the government be persistent. Alberta Environment should not let this strategy languish. The government of Alberta must continue to pursue and support the development of an evolving provincial water strategy based on the Water for Life model and continue to place considerable emphasis on collaborative approaches involving an ever-widening circle of interested stakeholders and public participants.

It was also recommended that the strategy be modified to include a balanced portfolio of measures for managing further water scarcity. Given the historical record and projections of future climate change, the province needs to adapt to the threat of droughts that could last ten years. This means the portfolio of adaptations should include water conservation, storage (both surface and ground), conjunctive use of ground and surface water, water reuse and other appropriate measures. The strategy should also make a commitment to the support of applied and basic research and ongoing programs of monitoring that will address specific problems, fill knowledge gaps and become the platform for developing high-level professional water management capacity. It is not enough to talk about what is known about the province's water resources. Knowledge has to lead to action. Policy objectives need to be translated into implementation targets that can be monitored, measured and compared. Targets should be modified over time as part of a learning process that specifically incorporates expanding knowledge and changing social preferences. To make this happen, the government has to listen and act upon the recommendations of stakeholder groups. Water governance must remain open, transparent, accountable and effective, and outside reviews must be undertaken periodically to assess the extent to which partnerships remain effective; participatory processes remain functional and all processes of governance remain accountable.

Monitoring networks for assessing the quantity and quality of both surface and groundwater will need to be expanded and strengthened in Alberta and throughout the West. Monitoring networks and indices for assessing ecosystem health also need to be developed and implemented. The habit of cutting monitoring programs whenever budgets are trimmed must end. Monitoring networks need to be maintained over time and be sufficiently dense to allow trends to be measured and analyzed and to permit early detection of contamination episodes.

More recognition has to be given to Alberta's upstream riparian responsibilities. It is fundamental to the success of the strategy that current agreements with other provinces and with the federal government may need to be modified and updated in response to changing circumstances. Interjurisdictional collaborations, with shared responsibilities for the management of water resources, must be created to oversee the development of databases for transboundary watersheds and aquifers and to facilitate the collection and exchange of data and information. It is equally important that institutional arrangements be developed to ensure that watershed and aquifer management plans are reconciled and are compatible with one another. The strategy will ultimately need to include a list of implementation instruments that could be used to achieve each policy objective. The strategy should also encourage the development of new and innovative mechanisms and collaborative tools for achieving its goals.

Finally, responsibility for provincial water management cannot be held by just one government department. At present at least 14 different government departments have responsibility for some element of water management. As Manitoba recognized when it created a separate water stewardship ministry, too many chefs can actually contaminate a broth. All provincial ministries must become mindful of policies and activities within their respective domains that involve or affect water resources, and must harmonize their actions with respect to the protection of water quality and availability. If this is to happen in Alberta, this recommendation will require commitment and support from the Premier and the highest levels of the provincial government. Such a commitment is necessary, however, if Alberta's Water for Life strategy is not to become just one more good idea that failed.

Trending toward Solution of the Global Water Crisis

PETER GLEICK, A HIGHLY REGARDED international water policy expert, summarized the important lessons and directions that emerged from the 2006 Rosenberg Forum. Dr. Gleick urged the water policy community to move away from ideology and fixed ideas with respect to addressing water supply issues globally. He offered two examples. First, there is tension between the position that water should be treated as a human right and the position that it should be treated as an economic commodity. The forum put into relief the futility of this argument. The quantities of water needed to sustain life should be considered a human right, while quantities in excess of that might appropriately be subject to commodity-like approaches. Second, the debate over whether water management should be a public or private endeavour is similarly unproductive. The dispute masks the fact that both private- and public-sector entities have records of success. Each has application in appropriate settings.

Gleick emphasized the conclusion of the forum that water challenges globally cannot be successfully addressed without better communication among scientists, policy-makers and the public. It is not enough just to do research. Scientists will need to find better ways to communicate with policy-makers and with industry. Policy-makers will have to make a genuine effort to understand science and what scientists can contribute to policy development. And all parties must do a better job of communicating accurately and effectively with the public.

Another important conclusion that was reemphasized in the 2006 Rosenberg Forum is that economic development and human well-being are not inextricably linked to increases in water use. Dr. Gleick noted that water use in the u.s. has dropped dramatically during a period of unprecedented economic growth. There are a variety of explanations for this phenomenon, but it is largely due to improvements in the efficiency with which water is used.

A major conclusion of Forum V was that mounting evidence about climate change means that water planners and managers cannot simply rely on existing models and policies. Old assumptions that the climate is unchanging are no longer adequate, and water planning and management will have to be adaptive and flexible in response to climate-related impacts. Climate change is leading to new and difficult challenges to sustainable water management and use globally. A lesson for us is that we may want to catch up with the rest of the world in recognizing that threat as just one of a number of problems we will need to address.

To this end, it will also be important to integrate issues and avoid jurisdictional and institutional isolation. Sustainable water solutions inevitably come from the merging of a variety of approaches. These approaches include adaptive watershed management, the integration of water and land use policy, inter-disciplinary solutions, and analysis of "soft" as well as "hard" approaches to water management problems. This suggests that we cannot rely solely on engineering to resolve the problems we are creating for ourselves; we will have to change some of our habits.

Discussions at the forum also revealed that national and local water problems are growing in scope and magnitude, and that there is little difference between the water problems of the developing world and those of the developed world. Important progress is being made in finding solutions, but the prospect of population and economic growth around the world mean that much more progress is needed.

New ways to tackle old problems are needed but it will also be crucial to understand and address emerging new problems and, more importantly, to anticipate them. We live in a period of very rapid change, and new paradigms in the management and use of water will have to be developed in response to such change. This is clear in Canada as Canadians witness the fact that water is entering Canadian consciousness as it never has before. There is indeed an emerging global water crisis, and Canadians are not immune to its impacts.

≈

Seven Lessons from Forum V

THERE ARE PERHAPS SEVEN overarching lessons Albertans and Canadians can learn from the fifth biennial Rosenberg International Forum on Water Policy, held in Banff in the fall of 2006.

First, Canada is not as advanced as it might like to believe in terms of public policy relating to water supply and quality assurance. There are issues of equity; inefficiencies associated with jurisdictional fragmentation of responsibility and accountability; an absence of reliable and commonly useful data; and widespread examples of inadequate foresight and management of water in the context of other forms of resource development. There are many gaps in federal and provincial water management policy that need to be filled. The country needs to move past its own myths of limitless water abundance to create a new, national water ethic based on conservation and different formulas for valuing water as a resource in its own right.

Second, compared to other places in the world, there is not yet a water crisis in Alberta or in the Canadian West. But Alberta in particular has all the makings of one. These elements include heavy agricultural reliance on water, rapidly growing populations, increased water demand from cities and industry, reduced flows in important watercourses, and unpredictable climate variability.

Third, there are others from whom Canadians and Albertans can learn. On the pre-forum field trip to the Columbia Icefield, Don Lowry of EPCOR was introduced to Abdel Metawie, who is chairman of the authority that manages the waters of the Nile River in Egypt. Dr. Metawie presented Don with one of his business cards. On it was the first symbol used by the water authority when it began managing the river. Beneath the symbol were the words "Managing water since 4241 BC" We were astounded. Dr. Metawie reminded us that the Egyptians have been managing the Nile for 6,000 years. It is reasonable to suspect they have something to teach us.

There are others from whom Canadians and Albertans can learn. Canadians should vigorously pursue access to global knowledge and experience, so that we do not make the same mistakes others have made. The old saying is true: every time history repeats itself, the price goes up.

The fourth lesson is that though it is highly significant in the Canadian context, Alberta's Water for Life strategy is not unique. Approaches similar to this have been explored in many other countries, with varying degrees of success. It could become unique, however, simply for becoming fully implemented. Such implementation will require political support and appropriate funding.

The fifth lesson is that, politics aside, the measure of Canadian water management success will be determined not by what is said but by what is actually done in support of Water for Life and other water management initiatives.

The sixth lesson to emerge from Rosenberg Forum v is that Alberta and other western provinces presently have the resources to go right to the front of the world queue and get the management of water right.

The final lesson is that the longer policy-makers in water-scarce areas like western Canada wait to change their water management frameworks, the more investment there will be in current systems and the more difficult it will become to make needed changes. The western provinces should move now while there is still slack they can take up in their systems and before there is real crisis.

The world is watching. As Leith Boully, an Australian water policy expert, said at the conclusion of the forum, "Because of our current good fortune, Canada has a greater obligation than other countries to act soon, and appropriately."

Four: Reading the Wind: Reframing the Climate-Change Debate

≈

A Case for Reinterpretation of the Climate Issue

IF IN THE FUTURE WE LOOK BACK to a turning point in our history at which it might have been possible to correct a false direction in our global response to the climate change threat, the period in which we presently live could potentially be that point. It is possible, given the potential for compounded impacts associated with feedback mechanisms linked to global warming, that the juncture at which we currently find ourselves will be revealed as being several orders of magnitude more significant than any in our species' history, except perhaps for that fork in the road that led to our mastery of fire or the birth of agriculture and industry.

In the interpretation of the human and natural history of the Rocky Mountains we have faced similar junctures before, though none quite as significant. I am reminded, for example, of how differently we might think about where and how we live had the door not suddenly closed on accurate and sensible interpretation of the influence of the landscape on the psyche of travellers to the Rocky Mountains of Canada in the late 19th century.

That turning point, Terry Abraham suggested in his book *Mountains So Sublime: Nineteenth Century Travellers and their Eyewitness Accounts of the Rocky Mountain Wilderness*, revolves around the writings of the Irish aristocrat William Francis Butler. Published in 1872, Butler's *The Great Lone Land* offered a first-hand account of an expedition to the Red River and other travels and adventures in western Canada. The book was an instant classic because of the beauty and clarity of its landscape description. Such descriptions were utterly new.

Initially, the landscapes of the West as described by early travellers were too fantastic to be believed. Further exploration appeared to support this claim. It was soon argued that the landscapes of the West were, in effect, beyond the power of language or art to reproduce. Sophisticated visitors proclaimed the grandeur of landforms such as the Rocky Mountains as simply being beyond description. As the nature and character of these places were beyond words, everyone gave up trying. Except William Francis Butler.

Butler is important because he understood the huge intellectual challenge the Canadian West posed to those who would experience it and later attempt to describe those experiences in words. He knew this could only be done by creating a new descriptive vocabulary, new comparisons, analogies and similes.

Butler went so far as to attack the uninspired interpretation of the Western wilderness. He challenged those who loved the landscape to "put down their wooden words" in order to find new ways to represent the natural glory of place. In his own writings Captain Butler never ceased in his quest to describe the ineffable. He never let up in his efforts to create descriptions and interpretations worthy of the places he visited and people he met. He never stopped trying to transcend the "already seen" and "already said" in his experiences and interpretations.

For this reason William Francis Butler is seen in retrospect to represent an important divide in the literature of the Canadian West. His work marks a transition between writers who attempted to expand the language and perceptual capacity that is at the heart of vibrant interpretation of place, and later writers and artists who merely used the landscape to talk about themselves.

The point could be made that if we wanted to go back to that point in the description of the landscapes of the mountain West to a place where our literature and interpretation took a wrong turn toward cliché and meaningless self-reference, we could go back to William Francis Butler. Unfortunately, it is unlikely that the average person or even anyone presently working as a professional in the field of natural and human history interpretation is going to rush back to the now-antique forms of description so favoured by Captain Butler and somehow put us on the right track. Butler's trail is cold. Besides, we cannot turn back now even if we wanted to. We are faced with crucial historical junctures of our own. There are turning points in our relationship with place confronting us right now that demand our fullest attention.

Going back to William Francis Butler we realize that all we lost by handing over the interpretation of the mountain West to railway and advertising interests was the direction of one stream of our literature. The implications of the turning point we face with global warming are far more significant. We stand to lose not just what is relevant about the little real literature that connects authentically to place, but place itself. We stand to lose the elements of where we live that are the foundation of our identity and prosperity.

With this threat before us it would not be an exaggeration to say that at no point has there been a time in our history when it has been more important to know where we went wrong and to start over again moving in the right direction. The climate change issue allows us an opportunity to find our way back to where our powers of description and interpretation began to fail us in our efforts to prevent what is happening to us now. We can find our way back from specialized knowledge and advocacy to the point at which knowledge most fundamentally informs values and values inform action. We have the opportunity to go back to the very point at which science and politics rode off toward their separate sunsets. We can go back to the point in our history where the positive and the normative ceased talking. We can return to the beginning of the climate argument to build a new bridge between science and public understanding that leads to right action.

Whether we want to or not, climate change will force all of us to become more global in our perspectives. We no longer have any choice about thinking globally and acting locally. In this context, mere knowledge is not enough. We need to know not just what the emerging science of climate change is telling us, but what it means. We need to go beyond the sharing of facts to the interpretation of meaning, the calculation of consequences and the advancement of actions that will allow us to get beyond the hand-wringing stage of dealing with this threat and into the domain of public action. For this reason, I believe there has been no turning point in history when effective knowledge translation has been needed more than now. What we need is a William Francis Butler to appear in our time to stimulate new and creative thinking about the climate challenge.

Nearly 150 years ago, William Francis Butler began pushing Canadians to transcend the "already seen" and "already said" in their descriptions of place. He demanded that those who followed in his footsteps work tirelessly to imagine and then create a new descriptive vocabulary of the West. He called for vivid comparisons, evocative analogies and energized metaphors that put the wonder of the West into new relief — exactly what we need now.

Butler believed that the Canadian West was one of the last places in the world where people could be shaped by place rather than the other way around. For Butler our landscapes were simply too amazing to allow them to become merely vehicles for talking about ourselves. Perhaps it is time to revisit Butler's concerns and to take up his challenge. Do not expect this to be easy, however. The climate change issue is not easy to grasp, let alone interpret. And as Walter Alvarez has pointed out, we should expect resistance to whatever we offer as interpretation, no matter how brilliantly it may be articulated.

Dr. Walter Alvarez is the University of California geologist who became famous in the 1980s for his groundbreaking work in determining what caused the demise of the dinosaurs. It was Dr. Alvarez who identified the meaning and significance of the thick layer of iridium-rich ash that has been found worldwide at the boundary between the Cretaceous and the Tertiary eras. Over the course of many years, and many bitter academic battles, Alvarez and his colleagues were able to prove that this layer of iridium was the result of a global catastrophe that resulted in the extinction of the dinosaurs. In time, Alvarez was able to locate the actual impact point in the form of an immense crater at Chixulub (*cheek*-shoe-lube) in the Yucatan region of Mexico.

At the close of a most engaging conversation, I asked Dr. Alvarez if he thought that the same intense rigour and fiercely focused peer review and criticism that attended his hypothesis of catastrophic contingency at the close of the Cretaceous would be applied to the science associated with climate change. As Alvarez is a geologist who understands rapid climate change, he did not hesitate in answering. He made it very clear that, though it was bitterly contested, his meteorite theory of dinosaur extinction did not socially or economically affect the lives of anyone outside the scientific community, in which it is customary to fiercely debate and test such ideas. The climate change issue, on the other hand, could directly affect the livelihoods of millions of people and the lifestyles of billions more. Expect the debate and criticism, he said, to become commensurately difficult. "Be prepared," he said, "the debate will be bitter."

≈

Reading the Wind in Canada

THE QUESTION WE MIGHT ALL ASK IS THIS: Who is going to sort all this out? How are we going to get enough people working together to properly frame the climate-change problem so that we can understand and address it? That the function of translating what we know into action is seldom being performed by researchers themselves suggests that an important role exists for those who can help to build a better bridge between scientific research outputs and public education inputs so that hard-won knowledge can be translated more readily into public policy decisions that lead to effective action. An entire professional field awaits creation around the urgent need for thoughtful, accurate and inspiring knowledge translation and interpretation of the climate change issue.

What happens to water will be the most obvious and immediately observable impact of climate change. The management of water resources in Canada is presently in the secure hands of the engineering field, which generally doesn't think much of non-engineers who bumble their way into water supply and other related issues. This is becoming a troubling situation in that we appear to be much better at listing potential impacts than we are at imagining consequences. We are better at engineering than we are at actually adapting. We are so good at engineering, in fact, that it is difficult to feel we have anything to worry about. This has led us in the direction of complacency. The public cries out, "The climate is changing! The climate is changing!" Government response is tempered by generations of reliance on engineering solutions: "Yes, yes, we know," they respond drolly. "We'll get to it."

There is a growing number of people Canada and in the world, unfortunately, who believe that government isn't getting to this issue fast enough. The situation with respect to climate change appears to be evolving far more quickly than we expected and the challenge of addressing climate-related issues appears to be getting more complicated every day.

The rest of the world is not as complacent about the issue as we are. Following are three quotes I captured during a 2007 visit to Europe to learn more about how members of the European Union are addressing water and climate issues.

I have been in Berlin for sixty years. It used to be that winter
lasted six months. Now we don't get snow and this year
there was no winter at all.

> — Pavel Podsadny, taxi driver
> Berlin, Germany

Winds of extraordinary velocity are becoming more
common. Recently winds of 217 kilometres an hour were
recorded in the Czech Republic. In January of 2007, wind-
storms of exceptional intensity and duration felled some
10 million cubic metres of wood as windfall in our region
alone. It seems that records for wind speed seem to be
broken almost every year.

> — Petr Kapitola, forest entomologist
> Prague, Czech Republic

We face serious water scarcity. Places that have adequate
water are likely to have productive agriculture. Those that
don't have enough water for agriculture had better hope
they have enough water to keep their landscape together, at
least to the extent that they will be able to support tourism.
Those places that can't may no longer be habitable.

> — The Hon. Jordi William, former
> Minister of Agriculture of Catalonia

Looking at what is happening elsewhere, I am afraid I simply
do not believe that emerging circumstances relating to climate
change will not result in increased tensions and even conflict
between those who demand greenhouse gas emissions and those
who have to make up or pay for them. This will be particularly
so if we, as one of the world's greatest polluters, really do need
to reduce carbon dioxide emissions by 70 to 80 or 90 per cent
to address the global warming threat, as some have proposed.
I simply can't see how we can avoid conflict in North America
over the issue, especially if we fail to frame the problem properly.
Even if we ignore for a moment the debate over the extent that
humans contribute to the problem, climate change can hardly be
classified any longer as just an environmental problem. It used to
be that, but it has become much more. Climate change impacts
relating especially to water have already begun, in tandem with
other human impacts, to alter the very foundation of where and

how we live in the Canadian West. At present, we have no idea where it will all end.

Few Canadians fail to notice that when the temperature rises in the spring, everything seems to happen at once. It stops snowing and begins to rain. Trees come into leaf, birds arrive, animals come out of hibernation and insects appear seemingly out of nowhere. People's dispositions and character change.

As we push the mean global temperature ever upward, the same thing will happen. Everything will occur all at once. We just don't know what. In precisely the same way, global warming has the potential to blossom all at once out of the environment as an economic threat, a social disruption and a political nightmare of a magnitude we have never faced on such a scale before.

Saying we don't have to worry about this because our climate has changed before and we survived just fine ignores important contemporary realities. But that hardly counts as an excuse not to act on what is happening now. That the climate has changed in past geological epochs is a given. While humans have certainly survived significant climate change episodes in the past, there are huge differences between then and now. Climate change should not be considered separately from other impacts we have already imposed on our planetary life-support system. Global warming is just one more cumulative effect superimposed upon many others. Seen in this context, we begin to see that we are in fact very vulnerable. Never before has there been so many of us. Never before have all the habitable places been so fully occupied. Never before has there been so much private property. Never before have our material demands been so great. Never before have our landscapes been so compromised. Never before in human history have our natural systems been so diminished and fragmented and so many species threatened with extinction. Never before in all of our history have we possessed so much immovable infrastructure and never before have we been so immobilized by legislative and legal precedent.

In the past, humans moved uphill in response to rising oceans. Or they moved inland or toward water. Today, we can't just get up and move like we did in the past. You just can't move a city. Besides, in the places worth living in, someone already lives where we would seek to go. If circumstances develop as projected, there will be few places we can all move to and no wild nature to which we might return. The biggest current problem, however, is that most of the projected climate impacts will be adverse if only because our economies and activities are not easy to change.

In this sense, the global warming issue has produced a perfect storm of population pressure, economic expectation, ecosystem decline, jurisdictional atomization and legislative precedent that could lead to serious unforeseen consequences. Tensions over who is at fault and what ought to be done are already mounting. A failure to respond effectively, not just to the problem but to how the problem is framed, could not only cost us our prosperity but also break down the current world order and force the establishment of a new geography of haves and have-nots in a rapidly changing and increasingly chaotic world.

It should be the responsibility of every thinking person in our society to make sure that things do not fall apart. Adaptation is within our grasp, but there is a lot to do and we are easily distracted from the task. To keep western Canada on track we need to do more to understand the challenge and unify our actions in support of appropriate adaptation. The first helpful thing we could do is establish a common understanding of what we know about the climate problem.

In this observer's estimation, the polls in Canada don't tell the whole story. Recent surveys say that 80 per cent of Canadians believe from their own experience that our climate is changing. In my experience, however, there is a disproportionate number of people in influential positions who do not buy the climate change story. One of the reasons for this is that we haven't told it completely or, for that matter, very well.

Many Canadians think climate change emerged out of a suddenly enemy sky in February of 2007, when our Prime Minister actually put the two words — "climate" and "change" — together for the first time in the same sentence. The fact remains, however, that we have actually known for a very long time about the threat posed by increased carbon dioxide in the atmosphere.

≈

Climate Science History 101

REMARKABLY, THERE IS A STRONG HISTORICAL LINK between mountaineering and the origins of climate science. The renowned Irish physicist John Tyndall was one of the most famous mountaineers of the 19th century. His mountaineering interests extended to his scientific work when he began to focus on the "wondrous factory" that is the atmosphere. Tyndall was the first to discover the heat absorbing qualities of both carbon dioxide and water vapour.

In 1859, Tyndall also predicted that a water vapour feedback mechanism initiated by carbon dioxide could dramatically increase the mean temperature of the Earth's atmosphere. The carbon dioxide concentration in the Earth's atmosphere during Tyndall's time was only about **290 parts per million**.

It is interesting to note that in the same year John Tyndall discovered the heat-absorbing properties of carbon dioxide a man named Colonel Edwin Drake drilled the world's first oil well in a little town called Titusville, Pennsylvania.

The earth-science community didn't pay much attention to either event. They weren't interested in climate per se. They were interested in ice ages. Ice was all the rage in the late 19th century.

In 1896, the famous Swedish physicist Svante Arrhenius speculated that ice ages came and went in some sort of dance with the amount of carbon dioxide in the atmosphere. Following on the heels of John Tyndall, Arrhenius posited that crucial changes took place in the amount of water vapour in the atmosphere as temperatures rose and fell. He was also among the first to describe what would later be called the Earth's atmospheric "greenhouse" effect and its consequences for global warming.

In his famous paper entitled *On the Influence of Carbonic Acid in the Air upon the Temperature of the Ground*, which he published in 1896, Arrhenius made the following astounding claim: "A simple calculation shows that the temperature in the arctic regions would rise about 8° to 9°c if the carbonic acid (known today as carbon dioxide) increased 2.5 or three times its present value."

In the 1920s, a Serbian scientist, Milutin Milanković, proposed that variations in the orbital pattern of the Earth were the likely cause of ice ages. The influence of such slight changes, however, didn't jibe at the time with the established notion of four major historic glacial periods. They do now.

In 1923, the average concentration of carbon dioxide in the Earth's atmosphere was **304 parts per million**.

It wasn't until the big droughts of *the 1930s* that anyone began looking seriously again at how climate change could ultimately affect the course of empire and the future of civilization. The Dust Bowl catastrophe that wiped out 250,000 farm families on the Great Plains got everyone's attention.

Gradually people began to see anomalies in the climate record. *In 1938*, an amateur climatologist named Guy Stewart Callendar stood before an astounded Royal Meteorological Society in London, England, and explained that his hobby consisted in collecting weather statistics. Moreover, his numbers indicated — more thoroughly than anyone else's — that the atmospheric temperature of the Earth was rising. Callendar also claimed to know the cause. He argued before this august scientific body that the burning of millions of tons of fossil fuels was warming the planet. A fairly significant war stood in the way of Callendar's revelations.

In the 1950s, Wallace Broecker, later of the Lamont-Doherty Earth Observatory, published the first speculations that the Earth's climate may be subject to much more rapid swings than had previously been believed.

In 1952, the average concentration of carbon dioxide in the Earth's atmosphere was **312 parts per million**.

In 1956, Gilbert Plass, at the time a weapons research scientist at Lockheed in California, discovered that increased carbon dioxide concentrations in the atmosphere would affect the amount of radiation that escaped from the Earth's surface into space. Plass announced that, according to his calculations, human activity would raise the average global temperature "at the rate of 1.1°C per century." Plass had no way of knowing that CO_2 concentrations would rise as fast as they have.

In 1957, Roger Revelle at the Scripps Institution of Oceanography in California discovered that carbon dioxide generated by human activity is not readily absorbed by the world's oceans, but lingers in the atmosphere. Revelle concluded that the amount of carbon dioxide in the Earth's atmosphere would gradually rise over the next few centuries and then level off, with a total increase of about 40 per cent over 1957 levels. He didn't worry that much, however. He thought the 21st century was a long way off.

In 1960, an American named Charles David Keeling initiated the longest-running carbon dioxide concentration baseline on the planet at an observatory on Mauna Loa in Hawaii. When Keeling began collecting his data, the atmospheric concentration of carbon dioxide was **315 parts per million**.

In 1963, an American astrophysicist named Walter Roberts demonstrated that aircraft were beginning to affect climate on heavily travelled routes by introducing large volumes of water vapour and aerosols at high altitudes, which induced cloud formation. Roberts dissuaded the u.s. government from investing in supersonic passenger and transport planes, for fear they would introduce water vapour and other exhausts into the high, thin stratosphere, where natural aerosols were rare and any new chemical would linger for years. Meanwhile, the Europeans went ahead with the Concorde. In 1963, the average concentration of carbon dioxide in the Earth's atmosphere was **319 parts per million**.

In 1973, the average concentration of carbon dioxide in the Earth's atmosphere was **329 parts per million**.

In 1975, concerns about the upper atmospheric effects of jet aircraft led to research into the concentrations of trace gases in the stratosphere. This research led to the frightening discovery that the Earth's ozone layer was threatened by chlorofluorocarbons, or CFCs.

Thirty years ago, *in 1977*, a World Climate Conference was held in Geneva at which 300 experts from over 50 countries concluded that an increase in carbon dioxide "may result in significant and possibly major long-term changes of the global-scale climate."

In 1980, acid rain was recognized as a serious problem. The average concentration of carbon dioxide in the Earth's atmosphere that year was **339 parts per million**.

In 1981, Jim Hansen of NASA's Goddard Institute for Space Studies in New York predicted that, considering how fast CO_2 was accumulating in the atmosphere, "carbon dioxide warming should emerge from the noise level of natural climatic variability" by the end of the 20th century.

In 1988, the United Nations created the Intergovernmental Panel on Climate Change (IPCC). In that year, the concentration of carbon dioxide in the Earth's atmosphere reached **350 parts per million.**

In 1991, the average concentration of carbon dioxide in the Earth's atmosphere was **355 parts per million.**

In 1992, Hurricanes Andrew and Iniki caused $19.5-billion in insured losses. Andrew's $15-billion insured loss wiped out all insurance premium income for the previous 20 years.

In 1998, there were a record 1,424 tornadoes in the United States. In 2004, there were 1,817.

In 2001, the third assessment of the Intergovernmental Panel on Climate Change reported there was new and stronger evidence that most of the warming observed over the last 50 years was attributable to human activities.

In February of 2007, the fourth IPCC report noted that climate change impacts were accelerating. The report also noted that human influence has already been substantial enough to affect the Earth's climate for the next thousand years. At the time the report was released, carbon dioxide concentrations in the atmosphere were about **380 parts per million,** up about 30 per cent since John Tyndall first speculated on the importance of carbon dioxide to atmospheric temperature way back in 1859.

Given the momentum of our current energy economy, carbon dioxide release could hit 12 billion tonnes a year, or **520 parts per million** by **2030.** As effective energy alternatives are only in the development stage, we are, whether we like it or not, wedded to fossil fuels as the foundation of our energy economy for the next decade or more.

In effect, we have already knocked back our second double carbon martini and are just awaiting the effects. What that means is that it will take at least a generation before we can seriously begin to mitigate climate change impacts. During that period we will have no choice but to watch the world heat up, and to live with the consequences. We have no other option but to adapt to the world we are in the process of creating.

≈

Understanding the Importance
of Climate Stability

IN CANADA, WE PRESENTLY ACT as though adaptation to the changes we are bringing about is going to be a simple matter of course. We view adaptation as a kind of societal product option — rather like ordering a sunroof on a new car. I personally do not see it that way. There is a very real chance that adaptation will be forced upon us. Go to Europe. See what is happening elsewhere. We are behind in addressing the problem. If we want to realize opportunity, then we have to get going.

Most Canadians believe it wouldn't hurt at all if the climate in Canada were a little warmer. While it is certainly true that the warmer winters we are enjoying are very pleasant, what is being missed in the climate debate in Canada is that most of us don't have any idea of the extent to which our society and its evolution have been a product of relative climatic stability. As one wit suggested, warmer western winters are gift wrap on a time bomb.

Something very basic about where and how we live is changing. The very stability of our climate is no longer something we can count on. While we cannot predict the exact rate and timing of projected changes, we do know that if climate change continues to occur at the rate at which it is already taking place, the past will no longer be a guide to the future. Businesses that are planning future growth and development based on the amount of water we have available to us today could very well be making a strategically dangerous mistake. All indications are that the past will no longer be a guide to the future.

Most Canadians have yet to understand the significance of this. Admittedly, it is a huge concept to grasp. It is also true that the public is being encouraged by special interests to deny the consequences of climate change. When we examine the credentials of many of the people that form the contemporary climate change Denial Machine, we find that their central qualification is often that they have made a career of opposing specific contemporary scientific views. That is not to say there is no place for contrary views. Humans, we know, are prone to collective delusion, and not everyone challenging the validity of climate science is misguided.

But the contrarian positions that garner so much public attention today are not helpful. Many of these people are simply cranks or industry hacks whose arguments stand in the way of legitimate forms of disagreement finding expression. If public discourse is carried by such people we are not going to get anywhere.

Professional public relations and lobbying are part of how business is done in our market economy. But there is a risk of being too good at it without keeping an eye on larger realities. We have all seen, for example, how effective lobbying ensured that North American automobile manufacturers remained exempt from legislation demanding more fuel-efficient vehicles. They have been so successful with their lobby that they have been permitted to keep producing inefficient cars and trucks even though it has hurt their business and our economy to do so. Because of persistent self-interest, North American auto manufacturers lost world domination of their own markets. We simply cannot afford to let climate-related issues lead to similar consequences in any of our other economic sectors.

No matter where we live, the potentially negative aspects of climate change are likely to be an unwelcome imposition on our lives. Global warming is already affecting water availability and quality. It is already affecting forestry and agriculture, recreation, tourism and human settlement patterns. Next it will affect real estate values, local identity and sense of place.

Many people still feel confused and helpless. There is no need to feel that way. This is a problem we can understand and address. We don't presently know what to do because we really haven't thought too much about what we *should* do. Until you get together to examine what the problem really is, you can't know how best to act. We have to get past all this hand-wringing. We have to get to thinking and then acting instead of worrying without thinking.

The first step in this thinking process is the acceptance that it may not be wise to ignore the problem. Try this: you are canoeing on the Columbia River. You are with three other people, for whom you care a great deal. One is your wife, one is your daughter and the other is your son. You are below one of the major dams on the river when you notice a wall of water approaching from a distance that might suggest that either a great deal of water has been suddenly released from the dam or perhaps it has burst.

Given your vulnerability it would be mad to say, "Don't worry, you don't even have to think about it — I just read a novel that said that dangerous dam releases never happen, and to the extent that they do, they are perfectly controlled."

How would your family judge you if you said, "We didn't sign any international agreement that would permit releases of this kind, and even if such an agreement were to come into existence, we could not permit its use or application to this or any other related situation"? Look at what has happened to the reputation of the United States for saying just that. Or how about this approach: how would your children's children respond if you were to be quoted as saying, in the midst of the dam failure, "I didn't personally release the water, so it isn't my problem. It wasn't me!"

≈

Ten Steps toward Acceptance and Adaptation

IN ORDER TO STIMULATE CREATIVE THINKING about the climate issue, the UN Water for Life initiative is inviting locals and visitors to consider ten steps that may allow us to come to terms with the climate change challenge in the Canadian West.

Step 1
Recognize that this matters, understand what the threat means to you, and commit to action.

O.K. If you still have doubts, try this: you are running a fever and it is getting worse. How long can you go before you go to the doctor? How sick do you have to become before you do something about it? How sick do you have to become before you can't do anything about it? We can still do something about this problem.

Step 2
Get the facts, share them, and get going.

The average person needs to know what is really going on or we will fail to act in time to take advantage of the opportunities that exist in adaptation. Please understand this: *there is no debate among practising climate science professionals that this is happening. It is not happening to somebody else, somewhere else. It is happening to us. Here. Now.*

One of the reasons we are so slow to act on this issue is that we believe technology will solve the problem for us. There is a good reason for feeling this way. The last two generations in particular have been spoiled by brilliant engineering and design. Good engineering solves our problems by proxy. It's amazing, really. If there is water scarcity, you don't have to use less water. Your high-tech tap will do it for you. Even though we face peak oil, you don't have to drive less. Your hybrid car will reduce your fuel consumption for you.

But sooner or later, in combination with other ecosystem impacts, climate change is going to demand that we alter some of our basic habits. We need everyone in to do that. To get everyone in, we have to do a better job of sharing what we know and we have to get going. There is no longer any point in delaying action until we sort out exactly how much of an impact we are making on our climate, as opposed to natural causes. It is a moot point.

Try this one: you find yourself on a narrow railway bridge that spans a chasm between two significant periods in human history. A train is approaching. It doesn't appear to be approaching quickly but you are not sure. Do you spend your time arguing whether it's a freight or a passenger train? Of course not! You get off the bridge and off the track.

It is not enough just to talk about doing something. We know enough to get started. We have to get past wishful thinking to action. It is not enough to talk about all the great innovations that are going to be available in the future that are going to make it possible to reduce carbon dioxide in the atmosphere. Claiming that a Chevrolet Volt is going to go 100 kilometres on half a litre of fuel doesn't mean General Motors has built it yet or that you are driving one right now. GM is presently building Hummers, and millions of people who don't need SUVs are still driving them. We cannot rely on the marketplace alone to address climate change issues.

We don't need to wait to get started, but we do need to understand science better.

Step 3
Build a functional bridge between science and local understanding.

Scientists need to get better at making their work understandable to others, and the public and politicians have to work harder to understand how science works and how to translate scientific research outputs into effective public policy and action.

We have to act on what we know. That means we have to build a better bridge between scientific research findings, public information and public policy choices.

Step 4

Harmonize local activities and programs with climate action goals.

We have to be careful not to make things unnecessarily worse by not taking the future into account in day-to-day planning decisions that affect our ability to adapt. Potential climate impacts need to inform all of our public policy and decision-making, starting at the community level, starting now. The first place to begin might be to determine where your water comes from, how much you use and how much you might have and need in the future. From this position of knowledge it will be possible to set conservation goals that will mesh with growth and development plans.

Step 5

Establish a regional climate agenda.

We would be wise to find out what we know and what we need to know to begin adapting to these climate issues. Then establish a plan for filling in knowledge gaps and building consensus on the best ways to adapt.

The Canadian Columbia River Climate Change Dialogue publication developed by the Columbia Basin Trust is an example of an excellent way to initiate regional climate change adaptation processes.

Step 6

Understand and appreciate current misunderstanding and self-interest and expect resistance.

At climate forums throughout the West, there always seems to be someone who shows up — often uninvited — during the last hour of a three-day event with an article in hand that says that somewhere in the world glaciers are growing. "See, you fools, they are not shrinking, and that means climate change is just an extremist environmentalist plot!"

The point here is that not everyone is going to be well informed on this issue. Not everyone's motives will be pure. Many people want to express opinions without having to do the work that would give their opinions meaning and value. But there is also something else going on here. Canadians often trust their myths more than their own eyes. One such myth relates to the limitless abundance of Canadian water. It is not going to be easy to leave outmoded myths behind. We have to be patient with one another and work together toward a common vision of what we see and what we ought to do.

Step 7

Recognize and bridge the difference between positive and normative claims.

We need to recognize the differences between science and politics. Science and politics operate on very different rules with very different aims. For this reason, scientists and politicians often have great difficulty communicating effectively with one another.

Walk in and say good morning to a scientist and she will likely check her watch. Walk in and say good morning to a politician and he will likely look around to see who agrees. Science and politics are different. One is a positive domain in which proof counts for everything; the other is a normative domain in which values and perspectives count for more than strict facts.

Whether we like it or not, both science and politics are necessary in a world in which we value knowledge but remain pressed to make hard choices on how limited resources and benefits are to be shared.

Neither science nor politics is going to change anytime soon. We need to build better bridges between understanding and action. If we don't, we could end up making the biggest mistake civilization can make: that is, to fail to adapt to climate change impacts even though we have the knowledge and the desire to do so.

Step 8

Build effective partnerships with organizations with similar climate-related needs and agendas.

We are not the only people in the world with serious concerns about climate issues. We are not the only ones who will be affected by it. No one is going to resolve this problem in isolation. It will be prudent to find out what others are doing and what we can all learn from each other.

Step 9

Carefully and respectfully build public-policy bridges at influential local, regional and national levels

We find ourselves in a very difficult situation with the climate problem. It is becoming crucial to decide how we are going frame this challenge. On one level we could make this very personal.

We could frame the problem as Ross Gelbspan did in his introduction to the book *Feeling the Heat: Dispatches from the Frontline of Climate Change*, which is to say that what we are facing is "a titanic clash of interests that pits the ability of this planet to support civilization versus the survival as we know it of the oil and coal industry, which is one of the largest commercial enterprises in history." While I greatly respect Gelbspan, one might ask where an adversarial debate like this is going to get us.

Another option is to transform a need into a virtue. We can frame climate change as a rare opportunity to improve the design, function and effectiveness of all of our major institutions all at once.

We need to decide whether we are simply going to get mad at one another and start fighting or are we going to face the problem together. We don't have much time for the former, and besides, the six-gun era of the West is a thing of the past. Or is it? It is time to decide, consciously, how we are going to frame this problem and then move toward the opportunity this issue presents.

Step 10

Embody our society's need to be positive and persistent while being flexible and adaptive

Providing that we begin to act now, we can reduce potential conflict over climate impacts, which if not addressed could be substantial by 2030. We need to lay down a framework right from the outset that encourages positive dialogue and thoughtful consensus on appropriate strategies for adaptation.

It is therefore important that we begin now by being unfailingly considerate and positive in our outlook on our climate future. It is also important that we be flexible and adaptive to changing circumstances and knowledge about climate issues.

We also need to recognize constantly the complexity of the issue and the crucial importance of keeping up with science and with unfolding events related to understanding of climate impacts on our West. There will be surprises — but not all of them will be bad.

We Have Solutions Already in Hand
That Can Address the Climate Change Threat

MUCH OF THE RESISTANCE to responding to the climate issue in Canada relates to fears about what greenhouse gas cuts might do to the economy. The fear is that rapid cuts cannot be made without sending the country into recession. Careful examination of our past successes, however, clearly indicates that this does not have to be the case.

Below is a graph of the gross domestic product of the United States from 1900 to 2000, created by Dr. Peter Gleick at the Pacific Institute in California and presented at the Rosenberg International Forum on Water Policy in Canada in 2006. As Dr. Gleick pointed out, it shows what some economists love to see: exponential growth in the economy.

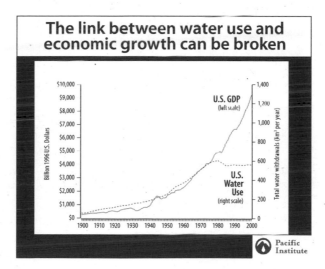

from
Dr. Peter Gleick,
Pacific Institute

The graph of total water withdrawals in the United States over the same period shows that in the first part of the century there was a lockstep connection between economic growth and population growth. Growth was inseparable from constantly increasing demand for water. But in the 1980s, these two curves split apart, and today the United States uses less water for everything than it

145

used in 1980. Out of this a new idea emerges: that we can actually break the link between economic growth and water use. This is a profoundly significant development, for if this can be done with something as basic as water use, then it should be possible to do the same with energy. This is, in fact, what we are actually discovering.

The graph below illustrates the same phenomenon occurring in the context of electrical energy demand in California. Once again we see the breakdown of what we thought was a lockstep process.

What energy efficiency can really do

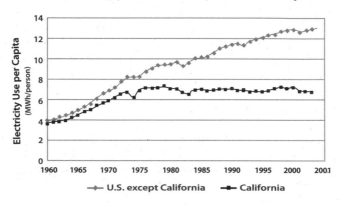

Modified from *Hell and High Water: Global Warming — The Solution and the Politics and What We Should Do*, by Joseph Romm. William Morrow, 2007.

This graph illustrates that energy use does not have to move in lockstep with economic growth. While economic reasons for addressing the climate change threat pale in comparison to the ecological motivations for acting, this graph illustrates that tackling the global warming issue does not necessarily have to result in the crippling of our economy as so many critics have suggested. We have been through this before. Banning DDT and CFCs did not wipe out the chemical industry. Despite dire warnings from utilities and coal companies that sulphur emission cuts would devastate the economy, these arguments proved unfounded. It is time to recognize that we have crossed a new and very different frontier. We have filled up the sky with waste. If preventing wastes and reducing pollution is a threat to our economy, we need a new kind of economy. Dealing with climate change will not bring about the end of the world. Properly orchestrated, addressing the global warming threat should allow us to save money over time through better energy efficiency and more productive water use. These are intelligent directions independent of the global warming issue, for they allow us to adapt to the fact that global oil production may have already peaked or will do so in the very near future.

When we talk about adapting to climate change, what we are really talking about is sustainability. Sustainability, however, is not as easy to define as productivity and profitability, which always seem to have priority over sustainability. But even though we don't have a firm definition of what sustainability really is, we know what it looks like. It looks like Joseph Romm's graph.

What the United Nations Intergovernmental Panel on Climate Change said in its Fourth Report, published in May 2007, is exactly what these two graphs are saying can be done. We have to break the lockstep between economic growth and energy consumption and carbon dioxide and other greenhouse emissions if we want to prevent climate change impacts from challenging our society's adaptive capacity. The UN report suggests there are a number of ways to do this and we are moving in the right direction. In other words, it can be done. So let's get doing it.

To achieve sustainability, we will need good technology. But technology alone will not get us there. We will also need the active support of everyone in our society to fulfill the terms and conditions true sustainability will demand. These need not be onerous terms, provided we choose them before nature imposes them upon us. There is a lot of work to do but it must be done if we are to create the West we want rather than having something we never imagined or desired forced upon us because we didn't act in a timely way in defence of what is important about where and how we live.

≈

Filling Climate Science Knowledge Gaps

THE MAIN GREENHOUSE GASES are carbon dioxide, methane, nitrous oxide and water vapour. Other greenhouse gases include hydrofluorocarbons, perfluorocarbons and sulfur hexafluoride.

These gases can be distinguished by their different capacities to trap heat and the length of time they persist in the atmosphere. Carbon dioxide, though it does not capture heat as well as methane, is the most abundant of the greenhouse gases and stays in the atmosphere for as long as a century. Methane is 23 times more potent as a greenhouse gas than carbon dioxide but is less profuse and lasts usually only a month in the atmosphere. Nitrous oxides are also powerful greenhouse gases but are less prolific in the atmosphere and more localized in their impacts.

Greenhouse gases trap radiation given off by the Earth and prevent it from escaping into space. A lot of this heat is stored in the oceans and redistributed by ocean currents. It is this process that accounts for the lag in the effect greenhouse gases have on mean temperatures, and why current greenhouse-gas-generated warming can be expected to last for centuries even if we were able to cut our emissions to zero immediately.

If you have noticed that September and October temperatures in the Rockies are often summer-like even though the days are shorter and nights cooler, then you have observed part of the greenhouse effect on climate in this region.

While public-relations campaigns mounted by the energy industry may make it appear that a lot of scientists and others still argue that climate change is not happening, there is an international consensus on both the fact that it is occurring and that humans are a big driver in what is happening to our atmosphere and global climate.

The Fourth Report of the Intergovernmental Panel on Climate Change, released in 2007, was the work of some 800 contributing authors, more than 400 lead authors from more than 130 countries and more than 2,500 expert scientific reviewers. This IPCC work represents the longest and most vigorously peer-reviewed research project in the history of science. There is no longer any debate among practising climate science professionals that climate change is happening and that we humans are one of its principal causes. It is not unreasonable to repeat that global warming is not happening to somebody else, somewhere else. It is happening to us, now. This, however, does not suggest that we know everything we need to know to mount an appropriate adaptive response to the problems we are beginning to face.

It is important to realize that though climate change symptoms are clearly and undeniably upon us, there is still a great deal we do not know about our atmosphere and what it might do as the Earth's temperature rises. Knowledge gaps constrain the design and implementation of appropriate instruments to deal with the effects of climate change. In order to determine the full range of global warming impacts we can expect in the Canadian West, we will need to invest in research that will fill in the gaps in our knowledge about climate dynamics in our region. There are a number of such blanks that need to be filled.

A good deal of our concern about climate impacts has emerged through sophisticated computer models of the climate called global climate models or general circulation models, commonly known as GCMs. We need to further examine the validity and uncertainty of global climate models by comparison of outputs among models and to other sources of climate information such as instrumental and proxy records of climate variability and change.

A number of scientific tools exist for plotting climate conditions backward in time, far beyond weather records that exist at best only for the last century. We can employ analysis of glacial advance and recession to tell us what climates were like in the past. We can also study lake and bog sediments, examine tree rings and analyze pollen. These tools also include ocean sediment records and records left in coral reefs, loess deposits and paleosols. If we want to go back even further we can analyze trapped air in ancient ice cores in Greenland or Antarctica. More sophisticated dating technologies such as radiocarbon and uranium series dating can also help us know what the climate was like in the past. All of these tools have been employed individually and together in the development of the climate models we have created to project climate change impacts in the future. We need to keep filling the gaps in this knowledge.

It would be very helpful also if we could apply other sources of climate information besides scenarios derived from global climate models, such as historical scenarios of climate change from the recent past, to the forecasting of future climate.

One of the reasons we are confident that humans are a principal source of current global warming derives from the fact that climate modellers can only reproduce current warming trends if they include the greenhouse gas emissions created by humans. If you exclude the effect of human beings on the atmosphere, then models show that there should be no warming or even a slight cooling, when in fact mean temperatures are rising significantly. More work has to be done, however, to determine exactly how much of the greenhouse impact can be attributed to humans as opposed to natural, cyclical processes. While we know the human contribution is substantial, perhaps as much as 75 per cent, we do not currently have the ability to exactly apportion climate change impacts to natural and human causes. This makes it difficult to differentiate with complete accuracy between global warming and natural long-term climate cycles. To fill this research gap we will need to do more to validate established climate impact scenarios by continuing to test their capacity to simulate past environmental change.

We also need to continue developing and applying methods of downscaling global climate models to develop scenarios of future climate at higher spatial resolution. What this means is that we need to create models that will tell us what will happen not just generally over a large area of the globe, but at specific locations.

In order to advance our knowledge of potential climate change impacts we need to further improve on the current generation of climate impact models by accounting for the adaptation of ecosystems to global warming and elevated CO_2 and the adaptation of social and economic systems to a changed climate.

Though we have developed reliable models of general trends toward change in our overall climate, we have yet to develop reliable models of climate variability and extremes. This is crucial, as it is these extremes that pose the greatest threat to our current infrastructure and societal order. Better understanding of projected variability and extremes, at the regional level in particular, will help us plan appropriate adaptive response to the global-warming threat. This will also help fill in another important gap in our knowledge: understanding the opportunities and vulnerabilities we will face, sector by sector, in our economy.

We are only in the early stages of being able to determine the economic costs of the potential impacts of climate change. More work needs to be done in differentiating between the impacts of climate change (general trends) and the impacts of climate variability (especially extreme departures from the trends). Research in this area will allow us to more clearly determine the net impacts of climate change through consideration of the extent to which human and natural adaptation will offset the potential impacts.

Another knowledge gap that needs to be filled is in evaluating and enhancing the adaptive capacity of our communities and our major institutions such as government and industry. Not all the impacts of global warming are going to be bad. We need to further explore the business opportunities provided by adaptation to climate change and, in particular, adaptation knowledge and technology transfer that will facilitate appropriate response to climate threats.

With respect to the mountain West, the most important gap we need to fill is in the development and improvement of models of the climate sensitivity of the alpine, forest, aquatic and grassland ecosystems, starting in the Rockies and extending outward through all of the watersheds in western Canada. Finally, we need to do a great deal more to translate climate change research outcomes into public policy and the planning of adaptation to climate change.

Clearly there is a great deal of work that has to be done if we are going to completely understand the climate change challenge and adapt effectively to the altered reality we are creating. To catch up with the rest of the world on this issue, it will be particularly important not to be distracted by information sources that aim to purposely mislead us about the extent of our existing knowledge or about the seriousness of this threat.

Spin and Counterspin: Confronting the Denial Machine

UNFORTUNATELY, MAINSTREAM SOCIETY is entering a debate that has already been in progress for many years and in which sides have become in some instances bitterly entrenched in their positions and have forgotten common interests in addressing the global warming threat.

One of the most important things we may be able to do at this time is to prevent ourselves from falling into already existing entrenched positions that lead to unproductive argument that further delays appropriate action on the climate issue. If we are to properly understand what is happening, what it means and what we should be doing to adapt to the circumstances that are emerging, we cannot afford to have the debate continue along the adversarial lines we have allowed to develop over the past two decades. We have to raise the debate out of its current "them versus us" entrenchment. We have to rise above the spin and counterspin to get to the heart of the problem. We have to move from a "do we have to" mentality with respect to climate issues to a "we can" affirmation of capacity and intent.

This is not a simple challenge. A great deal of expensive public-relations expertise has been applied to manipulating public opinion on the climate issue by corporations who can only sustain their current profitability by not having the pay the real cost of their externalities. Externalities are the public costs and social consequences associated with private actions. Greenhouse gases are the ultimate externality in that they are invisible by-products of wealth generation for which the public must later pay in terms of quality of their environment or directly in terms of costs associated with addressing impacts. Public policy intervention is, unfortunately, required in situations where externalities such as CO_2 begin to impose huge economic consequences on a society. Governments exist to ensure that the common good is served through such policies. Governments that do not act in service of the common good in such situations are not doing their job.

At present, at least seven different public-relations traps have been created to prevent the public from acting on the need to make polluters pay fairly for their externalities instead of merely taking the profits from generating these by-products and leaving the public to pay the costs either directly or in terms of a diminished quality of life. Each of these traps — and whatever new public-relations tactics that emerge with the aim of further obscuring the issue — must be carefully skirted if we want to avoid delaying understanding and action on this crucial global issue. Here are seven professionally developed public-relations manipulations that are presently being employed to stall action on climate change impacts:

Strategy 1:   **Deny there is a problem.**

Strategy 2:   **Discredit science and scientists that suggest there is a problem.**

Strategy 3:	**Blame current global warming solely on natural variability.**
Strategy 4:	**Press for intensity targets without carbon caps.**
Strategy 5:	**Champion new scientific hypotheses that do not implicate fossil fuels.**
Strategy 6:	**Acknowledge that global warming is happening but assert that it is too late to stop it.**
Strategy 7:	**Demonize those who believe in human-caused global warming as "environmental terrorists."**

It is doubtful that any of these arguments are going to get us where we need to be. The moment we are drawn into any one of these traps, the chance of making any meaningful progress through dialogue is much diminished. We cannot permit the climate change problem to be framed for us in these adversarial ways. We need to replace these arguments with a positive vision of the future.

Climate Change as the Foundation for a New Vision of the Mountain West

THE CLIMATE CHANGE CHALLENGE is an opportunity for us to rethink the construct of our society and move toward ways of living that will redefine our future. Nowhere is this more so than in the Canadian West, where it presently appears that anything goes, anywhere, any time. Things are changing here faster than we can comprehend them. Elements of place and culture are disappearing faster than we can mourn their loss. It is no longer a secret that we are destroying the very qualities of place that attracted so many to move here. It is gradually becoming clear to every thinking person that our current way of life is simply unsustainable. Like a person who lives an unbalanced life, we know that sooner or later what we are doing here will catch up with us. The dizzy spells that climate warming impacts are beginning to cause should put us on notice that big changes in the way we live will be necessary to prevent impending illness from robbing us of our vitality and future. Soon we will no longer be able to live as we have in the past. It is time to determine what will be possible in the future.

The climate change signal does not have to mean the end of everything meaningful about where and how we live in the West. What it does mean, though, is that we have to focus on the West we want to have before the choices presently before us evaporate in the rising heat of rapidly accelerating change. We need a new vision of the West at its future and ultimate best. That vision cannot be just an extension of the old pioneer vision of rugged individualists marking their geographical and political territories against the common good. If we continue in that direction then we will lose all of the qualities of place and culture that have made the West such an attractive place to live. What we need is to see our landscapes anew and reaffirm those elements of our way of life we want to endure. Over time, we will have to reposition the values we want to protect and celebrate within a new energy context.

We presently face many environmental, social, economic and political challenges globally as a result of the amount of energy we use. It is clear that we may be at or close to peak petroleum availability and that these resources will be less available and more expensive in the future. This does not mean, however, that we will not be wedded to fossil fuel use for some time yet. Given this fact, why don't we make it our society's goal over the next 50 years to find ways to sustain our quality of life while at the same time cutting our energy needs and reducing their greenhouse effects?

We know from what has happened in the United States and elsewhere that it is possible to break the lockstep link between economic growth and constantly increasing water and energy use. These are important breakthroughs that tell us we can address the climate change issue without destroying our economic foundations. We should be building on these breakthroughs. We could make this a measurably healthier, safer and more prosperous world in the future if we made it our society's single greatest priority to sustain our prosperity while at the same time improving our energy efficiency by 70 to 80 per cent by 2050. In so doing, we could improve our way of life, solve a great number of environmental problems and pave the way to a more sustainable future. If we were to commit seriously to this direction, the avoidance of climate change disruption could almost be viewed as an added bonus. Certainly, it would be an important bonus — one that would be expected from the outset — but it would emerge from a backdrop of wise long-term social and economic policy.

Rather than pointing fingers at one another, wouldn't it be wise to reframe the entire climate debate? Why wouldn't we start with something like this: what social and economic incentives could we create that would allow us to sustain our prosperity through redirection of our intelligence and industry toward doing more with less energy? What would happen if we were to focus our substantial research and public policy capacity? Imagine what we could do if we were to embark on a global project like the one that got us to the moon; if we were to really focus on cleaning up our energy sources and radically improving our energy efficiency. Why couldn't such an initiative become part of the foundation of the West we want? Certainly, it would be cheaper to do that than pay to reinforce or replace all our infrastructure to make sure it can withstand the far more energetic climate we are projected to have. Let's set the bar high. Let's set out to cut our greenhouse emissions by 80 per cent and improve our energy efficiency by something like a factor of 10. Let's make 2050 the date by which we want to have achieved our goal. Wouldn't that be far more productive than blaming one another for creating a global warming problem we all created?

To create a vision for the West we want, we will have to establish new forums that allow collaboration to rise out of the rut of unproductive conflict and self-interest that presently characterizes most of the current discussion about the direction we are taking toward the future. An enlightened dialogue on how to collectively adapt to climate change could serve as a new foundation for deciding on the West we want in the future. The creation of such a vision, however, will require disciplined leadership. As the u.s. philosopher Christopher Lasch put forward in his book *The True and Only Heaven*, visions are not established through rhetoric that defends established positions. Arguments are not won through the clash of dogmas. They are won through respectful hearing and careful, logical debate.

It is the act of articulating and defending our views that lifts them out of the category of opinion, gives them shape and definition, and makes it possible for others to understand them. Lasch maintains — correctly, I think — that until we have to defend our opinions in public, they remain half-formed convictions based on random impressions and unexamined assumptions. Only by subjecting our preferences and projects to the test of debate do we come to understand what we know and what we still need to learn. As every citizen who has ever stood up in a public forum understands, we come to know our minds by explaining ourselves to others.

Every citizen who has ever been active in a functioning democracy has also learned that the attempt to bring others around to our point of view carries with it the risk that we may adopt an opposing point of view. As Lasch points out, true dialogue demands that we enter imaginatively into our opponents' arguments if only for the purpose of refuting them. There is always the chance that we will be persuaded by those we sought to persuade. Because argument is risky, it is educational, but isn't education a principal goal of life?

Five: Future Landscapes in the Mountain West

≈

Our Greatest and Most Enduring Cultural Achievement

THAT THE WEST WE CARE SO MUCH ABOUT is under siege goes without saying. All that stands between us and further loss and diminishment is the intergenerational wisdom, the constantly improving science and the carefully evolving public policy that compose the foundation of our protected-places system, here and around the world.

While our wisdom in choosing to preserve large areas of the mountain West has been recognized widely, our reputation in other environmental areas is in rapid decline internationally. Because of our stand on climate change we have been found out. The huge difference between what we say about our concern for the global environment and what we actually do in support of the values we purport to hold is now being widely recognized.

In his 2006 book, *Heat: How to Stop the World from Burning Up*, George Monbiot points out that in Europe it is widely held that to doubt that anthropogenic climate change is happening you have to have abandoned any notion of science and reverted to some private means of understanding the world: alchemy, perhaps, or magic, or maybe comfort and greed.

Regarded in Europe as one of the most influential thinkers of the 21st century, Monbiot is disgusted with how the u.s. denial industry has been permitted to hijack common sense in the climate change debate. With characteristic clarity and wit, Monbiot explores the Faustian pact we have established with our energy needs, and works his way through the science that in his opinion clearly indicates the direction we have to go in reducing greenhouse gas emissions. Monbiot is not blind, however, to the impacts that emissions reductions might have on England and other European countries. His concerns reside not so much in the threat of direct impacts but the effect on prosperity that inaction itself will have.

Monbiot slams Canada for the failure of its good intentions and outlines the hypocrisy of blaming China for the world's inaction on the climate problem. He complains that one of the reasons we are reluctant to address the climate issue is that taking action will expose just how corrupt some aspects of our society have become. He goes on to offer a description of the world as it might be if we don't act on the problem. He concludes with a sobering analysis of our social structures that puts into relief the reasons why the global warming problem is going to be very difficult for a society like ours to effectively address. While coming out on the optimistic side, Monbiot does not let readers off the hook when they close his book. His arguments tend to linger and nag. This is one of the reasons why *Heat* is such an important work.

The climate change issue in Canada has been allowed to become less a debate about science than a debate about beliefs. In Europe the issue is framed differently. As renowned Swiss scientist Henry Baltes recently explained, "I don't 'believe' in climate change, because I don't need to. Belief is something that I need to address matters of faith and religion. There is no need to 'believe' in climate change like you Canadians seem to think. I *know* that climate change is happening. If you don't believe in climate change, then there must be something you don't fully understand about the concept of the thermometer. You Canadians do use thermometers, don't you?"

All that said, there is one environmental achievement in which Canadians can take great pride — even when travelling abroad. While some of us may be frightened to the core of our very being by the potential seriousness of the climate threat and the implications of our national and provincial denial of it, we can still remain justifiably proud of our system of protected places in Canada's western mountains. I for one am confirmed now in the belief that what four generations of passionate locals, thoughtful land managers, scientists, park wardens and rangers, and far-thinking administrators and politicians have created here is one of the greatest public policy achievements in the history of the Canadian West.

We may not have always known what we were doing or to what end our collective efforts might be aiming, but what we have created here — the Canadian Rockies World Heritage Site and the protected places that buffer and shield it — is a public policy accomplishment of global significance.

The major premise of this new historical perspective is that over the last 125 years Canadians have somehow managed to collectively recognize what they possessed in the mountain West and to act upon that recognition.

Instead of dividing the landscape into halves and then quarters and eighths until it was utterly diminished and lost — as is the Canadian custom — in the Rocky Mountains we somehow recognized the value of what we had, stepped back from destroying it, and slowly started putting it back together again.

This is different from what has happened elsewhere in Canada and in the world. I maintain that the mere act of restraint in saving what we already had may well be our greatest cultural achievement, one that will shape the country and its people for generations to come. This is more important than it may seem. The act of appropriation that created the Europeanized West we know today was a gradual process. The milestones that mark our relentless march across the continent have become important dates in our nation's history. While we celebrate them as heroic events, they can also be seen as hostile acts that accelerated the carving up of the continent and the selling off of what was not ours to sell.

The first act of jurisdictional division was the granting in 1670 of a fur-trade monopoly on all the lands whose waters poured into Hudson Bay. Anthony Henday is said to be the first to target the Rocky Mountains for European jurisdictional fragmentation, in 1754. David Thompson crossed the Rockies in 1807 to advance what was essentially a British claim. In 1846 the U.S. claimed the lower Columbia. In 1867 Canada was created. In 1871 British Columbia became a province. In 1885, the Canadian Pacific Railway was hammered through the Rockies. In 1905 Alberta became a province. In 1912 the Grand Trunk Pacific was completed through Yellowhead Pass.

In 1922 came the first roads. In 1939 the Rockies were formally fragmented by the Banff-Jasper Highway. In 1952 a highway and a pipeline were rammed up the Athabasca Valley. In 1962 the Trans-Canada Highway was punched through Kicking Horse Pass.

In 1977 the wide-bodied jet arrived on the scene, making it possible for anyone to go anywhere in the world in a day. There is now no place left that is not within a jurisdiction. There is no place that isn't known and no place that isn't owned. A national vision of a settled West has been fulfilled.

Our efforts to restore what we had damaged once we saw its great value are far less well known than the events that define development of the mountain West. But they are at least as important. These efforts began quietly with the creation of individual mountain national and provincial parks that were clustered around the Great Divide of the Canadian Rockies.

No one could have imagined at the beginning how remarkably important the creation of each element in this network would become. The first of these small reserves, as we all know, was Banff. Banff was followed in 1886 by Yoho and in 1907 by Jasper National Park. Mount Robson Provincial Park was created in 1913 and Mount Assiniboine in 1922. Kootenay National Park came along in 1923, followed by Hamber Provincial Park in 1941. Then the Second World War and its aftermath froze the creation of protected places until prosperity and increased mobility made it possible for more Canadians and their guests to see what they had.

Once the pieces were saved, it took us 40 years to recognize their great value, which was far more than the sum of their parts. The idea of recognizing the planetary significance of the remarkable features encompassed within this national and provincial park network first found expression in 1982. In that year the Burgess Shale in Yoho National Park in British Columbia was identified as one of this country's first UNESCO World Heritage Sites. In 1984 the four mountain national parks were together granted the UNESCO World Heritage Site designation. But that was only a prelude to a grander designation that was to follow six years later. In 1990 the three surrounding British Columbia provincial parks were added to the mountain national parks under an expanded designation that created one of the most remarkable and significant large-scale ecological and cultural reserves in the world.

What we had created is nothing less than one of the greatest collective expressions of the will to protect national heritage the world has ever witnessed. What we have done is amazing. Between 1885 and 1941, what was at first a patchwork of tiny and isolated protected places has grown together to become a contiguous system that now encompasses 2,440,568 hectares, more than 24,406 square kilometres of some of the most spectacular mountain landscapes in North America.

This is a meaningless number until one starts comparing the expanded area of the Canadian Rockies World Heritage Site to the size of sovereign states. This 9,423-square-mile natural mountain reserve is roughly twice the size of the states of Connecticut or Delaware or the countries of Lebanon or Kuwait. It is larger than Belize, Israel or Wales. This one World Heritage Site it is almost a third larger than Swaziland and almost 60 per cent bigger than Northern Ireland.

Beyond its sheer scale, perhaps the thing that is most amazing about it is that it essentially encompasses only one biogeographical and cultural region. And what a spectacular region it is. Few who have visited it, and none who have lived in it, would disagree that it is one of the world's most remarkable places.

We have accomplished this by making jurisdiction serve us rather than allowing it to divide us. We have made ourselves whole as a people by restoring the places that have in the past meant the most to our identity. And yet not all of us fully realize just what we have done.

The Canadian Rockies World Heritage Site encompasses four National Parks, three Provincial Parks, 13 National Historic Sites and four Canadian Heritage Rivers. If you examine a 1:50,000 map of the region, you will discover that within the Canadian Rockies World Heritage Site there are no fewer than 27 mountain ranges, 669 prominent peaks, 12 major icefields and some 384 glaciers.

These mountains are the water tower of the West. Within this combined reserve are a total of 44 rivers and 164 named tributaries, and only two of them are dammed. Four of the greatest rivers on the continent are born here. Within Site boundaries are some 295 lakes.

This World Heritage Site also encompasses 23 important mountain passes and at least 25 major airsheds. It encompasses three life zones and is home to more than 600 species of plants, 277 species of birds and 69 species of mammals, including at least a dozen different carnivores.

Within this territory are some 900 archaeological sites, some of which evidence the earliest presence of humans, dating from Early, Middle and Late Prehistoric times to the present. In historic times the landscape encompassed within the Canadian Rockies World Heritage Site was within the territories of at least 12 First Nations. Parts as well were the home of generations of Métis.

Currently there are four permanent communities within this World Heritage Site, with a total resident population of fewer than 20,000. So famous is this site that it is the destination of more than seven million visitors a year. So what's not to like? The future should be rosy, shouldn't it? But right now it is unclear.

What kind of future do we face? We get a partial answer to this question from the recent climate change vulnerability assessment done on the Canadian West by Dr. David Sauchyn and his team. The assessment is troubling. The climate in the region is warming at a rate that exceeds the global average. In Alberta, for example, mean annual temperature has increased in the range of 1°c to 2.5°c over the last century. We are already experiencing higher winter and nighttime temperatures. Snow and ice are declining as warmer, shorter winters convert snow to rain. Mean annual stream flows on the Canadian prairies have been decreasing since 1947.

Recent studies of spring snowmelt patterns and subsequent runoff volumes have demonstrated that some 30 per cent of the unregulated rivers in western Canada exhibit earlier spring runoff. It is anticipated that inevitable further temperature increases will affect precipitation timing, and higher mean temperatures will reduce soil moisture. Over time changes in precipitation are expected to have substantial impacts on water supply. While the southern Great Plains move in the direction of desertification, the climate in the Western mountains is also drying. This has huge implications for everyone who lives in the Rockies and its hydro-climatic shadow.

≈

Wind from an Enemy Sky

WHEN YOU THINK OF CLIMATE CHANGE, think of where the dawn's light first strikes at the beginning of the day. It strikes the tops of mountains. When you think of climate change, think also of where the sunlight touches the Earth most persistently, and that is where 24-hour light falls on the poles. Look to these places first for the impacts of change.

A temperature increase in range of 1°c to 6°c will cause dramatic changes in both these regions. We have already seen the kinds of changes that are happening in the Arctic. Similar changes are now happening widely in the Rockies. Vegetation zones in the mountain West are expected to shift upward by approximately 500 to 600 metres, or a range of about 1,600 to 2,000 feet, the equivalent of one vegetation zone in any given mountainous region.

The implications of these developments for ecosystem protection are profound. For the last century, the strategy for protecting global biodiversity has been to protect representative parcels of each important ecoregion. A study commissioned by Parks Canada predicted that many of our most treasured national parks and reserves may no longer remain within the biogeographical regions they were created to represent. Currently we have no structures in place to help us manage for such a development. Climate impacts may be the biggest challenge ever faced by Parks Canada.

It will not just be Canada that will face serious challenges in the protection of remaining intact ecosystems as a result of climate change. The foundation of the entire global protected places program, of which our mountain national and provincial parks are an important part, is that these representative areas will remain biogeographically stable. But the recently published Alberta climate change vulnerability assessment argues that global climate change impacts are already invalidating this assumption. The maintenance of global biodiversity will require us to aim to protect what will effectively become "a moving target of ecological representativeness."

Whole ecological systems are already advancing northward. Current ecological communities are fragmenting and regrouping into unpredictable new assemblages. The mountain West will be a different place by 2050.

Protecting existing landscapes will require that disturbances be managed; new stresses will need to be controlled and habitat modifications will likely be necessary to reconfigure protected areas so that they can survive emerging climate conditions. Biodiversity managers will have to figure out how to become "creation ecologists" as they learn to adapt to change. Meanwhile, snow cover, which is expected to diminish by 40 per cent in the Rockies, is already coming later to ski areas; mountain ecosystems are moving upward; invasive species are already appearing; and the glaciers are disappearing right before our very eyes.

But the changing character of ecosystems is not the only threat to protected places. Threats exist that will challenge their very designation. As landscapes are diminished æsthetically as well as ecologically by climate-related threats such as insect infestations and wildfire, and as other areas of the West become less habitable because of reduced water availability, upland regions are going to become ever more desirable places to live. People moving inland, uphill and toward water will not fail to see their growing value.

As it becomes clearer what precipitation will do and where the ground and surface water will go, we may well expect the greatest real estate play in the history of the West: the scramble to determine human settlement patterns in the face of growing climate change impacts.

As the West is reordered economically around growing populations and intensifying climate, all protected-places bets could be off. If we want to keep what we have, we will have to find ways to ensure that protected places participate in the creation of an economic as well as ecologically sound future.

The implications of these changes could dramatically alter our culture. As climate change impacts accelerate, as they almost certainly will do, governments will have to do a great deal more to ensure the reliable and predictable availability of the basic environmental goods and services that make our large cities and prosperous urban way of life possible.

A whole new global economy will emerge to provide the environmental services that nature at one time provided free on our behalf. The sheer scale and urgency of the project will require this to be so.

As greater climate variability and extreme weather become more common, this will require huge investments in infrastructure. Keeping things as they have been will become increasingly difficult. Managing our prosperity is going to take far more intensive intervention into ecosystem processes than ever before. More and more of our resources will have to be spent on managing natural, agricultural, forest and urban ecosystems so as to ensure the vitality of the basic processes that form the foundation of the environmental stability upon which our continued prosperity depends.

Imagine the directions we may be forced to take. These could include management of all wilderness areas toward defined goals of production of air, water, and species diversity; complete management of both surface and groundwater; integrated management of the energy, water and product inputs and outputs of agriculture and forestry; control of the composition, nature and behaviour of the Earth's atmosphere; and careful direction of global ecosystem change. The magnitude of the public policy changes that would be required in order to create the framework for such action on a global scale is more daunting than the challenge of creating a lasting international agreement on greenhouse gas reductions. Moreover, impacts are bound to accelerate.

We should expect further changes in the timing and nature of precipitation. We should expect shifts in agriclimatic zones and changes in the dynamics of our forests. We should expect an increase in the frequency and duration of violent storms. We should expect surprises and we should expect losses.

Though we are presently looking at an uncertain future, we have to see that there is a window of huge opportunity in this. Never before have we had a greater reason to create a vision of the West we want and to act on it. Never before has there been a greater urgency to get past the frontier free-for-all that once again defines our age to create a vision of what we want our West to be like at its future and ultimate best. "But it is impossible!" you will say, to move against the current of established economics and political direction. You can say this all you want, but history disagrees. Our greatest cultural and public policy achievements belie this argument. Behold the central Rocky Mountain ecosystem. We have done it once, and we could do it again.

≈

Creating the Future
by Affirming the Past

WE HAVE THE POWER STILL to create the future out of the past. By protecting the core of our mountain ecosystem — its very heart — we have laid the foundation for the next brilliantly orchestrated iteration of scientifically informed public policy in the mountain West. So what do we do?

It took about 55 years to lay the foundation for the protected area system that presently defines the ecological and cultural milieu of the mountain West. Because of the urgency created by population growth, landscape change and accelerating climate impacts, we don't have that long this time. We may have ten to 20 years at most   and the next five are the most critical.

There are seven things we might consider doing. To transform the West around our founding landscape values, we won't have time to complete one step before we advance to the next. We will have to move simultaneously on all fronts. Fortunately, some of these steps are already being undertaken. What we seem to lack, however, is a sense of urgency, and that is something we can either have now while we still have choices or later when we won't.

1. Acknowledge the true nature of our accomplishment

We have to think in larger terms about what we have, appreciate what we have done, acknowledge what we learned by doing it; and be unabashed in creating a vision for the future based on the foundation of past success.

Though we may not have consciously intended to do it — or even known we were doing it — the creation of the Canadian Rockies World Heritage Site and surrounding buffers is one of this country's greatest cultural achievements. It is a triumph of persistent, forward-thinking public policy.

This accomplishment should trump the history of development and fragmentation we presently celebrate as being so central to our identity in the West. Yes, the railway was important. Yes, the birth of tourism matters. Of course the development of the West defines us. But it's time to let some air out of these bloated icons. The real history — the one that will matter most — is not what we built, but what we saved. It is time to start saying that.

Breakthroughs in understanding the dynamics inherent in self-willed, self-generating ecosystem function will be as important to the future as the discovery of electricity was to the past. Those discoveries can only be made where such systems still exist. Our greatest future wealth may reside in the fact that we still have such places. In fact, it may be in such places that we learn how to save ourselves.

Most people who live in the West, particularly in cities, seldom think about the meaning or value of the larger ecosystem we have preserved. They have been trained by the tourism industry to think of landscape largely in recreational terms and to imagine that landscape in the context of the atomized jurisdictions into which we have divided them.

People think of hiking in Kananaskis or of skiing at Banff or Lake Louise. They think about hiking, biking and bears but they don't see the region as a functioning ecological whole that provides services without which our current quality of life would be hard to sustain. If you don't believe that, then think about how many dams and reservoirs we will need to build to replace the fact and effect of a vanishing snowpack.

I am prepared to bet that fewer than one visitor in ten to this region of the Rockies knows that seven of the parks that compose it have been together designated as a UNESCO World Heritage Site or why. My guess is that even fewer of them know what the central Rockies ecosystem is, or know anything whatsoever about the ecological services it provides to the region for free that we could ill afford to provide for ourselves. If we are going to save this region, we need to change that.

It is not enough, however, to tell people what we have. Because of the galloping impacts of population growth, landscape change and climate warming, what we have now will likely be history before we can explain what we lost. Knowing what we don't want isn't enough. What we need is a desirable vision of this world transposed over the next.

No one is going to create this vision for us. Federal and pro-vincial governments in Canada seldom lead but they will follow. The vision has to emerge locally. Whatever the future is going to be in this region, it is going to be created on the ground by selfless people working together toward a common vision and linked to one another through the Internet. Ideally, whatever we do next should be informed by science and founded on ecosystem values.

This isn't going to be easy. The mountain West is presently polarized very purposefully over environmental issues. We are going to have to get out of our intellectual, institutional and juris-dictional silos to create a larger vision, but once again the Central Rockies Ecosystem provides a means to do so. Let's look at what we have, not what we are missing. The compelling natural charac-ter of the Rockies drove the first iteration of the mountain West. It can drive the next.

2. We have to stop making things unnecessarily worse

Instead of trying to avert climate change, we are dismantling natural systems that serve as protection against climate extremes. At the same time, we are going full speed ahead in making land-scape changes that will not diminish but amplify climate impacts. It is as if we want to tempt fate. For every hybrid car we put on the road we unleash two Hummers. For every good decision we make we make two that are likely to make things worse in the future instead of better.

Sooner or later we are going to have to stop inappropriate development in the mountain West, if only because, in terms of energy and climate impacts, it is not sustainable. You don't have to look any further than a town like Canmore, Alberta, to see why. How long will we be able to justify heating 8,000-square-foot homes, especially if they are only occupied by weekenders flying in from London or LA. Because air travel introduces water vapour into the stratosphere, it has 2.7 times the greenhouse impact of ground travel. If air travel has to be cut by 60 per cent to reduce upper stratospheric pollution that accelerates climate impacts, what will happen then? The answer is obvious.

Definitions of sustainability in use today are almost completely self-referential. They refer principally to continuing our economies so we can maintain or improve our quality of life. Current sustainability measures do not even begin to address evolving ecosystem needs. We are kidding ourselves. What we are doing in the mountain West isn't sustainable. We have got to stop pretending that what we are doing has any lasting ecological value. At some point it would be wise to stop making things unnecessarily worse.

3. Link scientific research output to public education input

There is an urgent need to do a great deal of new research. But simply doing the research is not enough. We have to build a bridge between science and public understanding so that we can establish a common vision of the value of what we have in the context of global and climate change.

The Canadian Rockies World Heritage Site notwithstanding, conservation analysts like Stephen Meyer from the U.S. are now telling us that with huge human population growth the end of the wild in nature is inevitable. Our presence is so universal that humans have taken over the process of natural selection. We now choose what will survive and what will vanish. The world's remaining ecosystems are now being divided into intact systems and relic communities — biotic assemblages that have no hope of surviving over the long term without extensive human intervention. Relic communities are composed of ghost species, plants and animals with no hope unless we help them. Half the world's plants and animals are expected to become ghost species by the end of the century. Even now, our national parks and protected areas are the last places many ghost species have left to haunt.

Research tells us that outside and even inside these reserves, invasive, "weedy" species are being elevated to keystone species in almost every ecosystem and community. We are moving toward global species homogenization, a parking lot world of ravens and crows.

We are told that we have reached such a desperate point globally that we must concentrate on saving remaining whole systems and abandon trying to save biodiversity in a piecemeal fashion at its weakest points. We are told that, unfortunately, the world is now so diminished ecologically that we will have to let a great many relic biotic communities and ghost species vanish. We are cautioned now to know what we have and what it does and to anticipate what will be left when it's gone. We are told that function and not form should become the sole priority in a massive collective effort to fill in our ecological knowledge gaps in order to prepare for what will be lost.

We are told, finally, that though we are approaching the end of the wild as we knew it, it is not the end of life. Though a century of conservation effort has to a large extent failed on a global scale, we cannot give up, for what we have is still better than what could ultimately be. A degraded ecosystem, after all, is far superior to one that has collapsed. A degraded system can still provide ecosystem services we cannot afford to provide ourselves and without which our quality of life could dramatically fall.

On top of all of these cumulative impacts we must impose the uncertainty of climate change. Global warming will further undermine the planet's diminished biodiversity. This additional pressure will demand a complete reassessment of the purpose of our national parks and protected area trust. Parks can no longer be managed as static resources. Science is telling us that rather than imprisoning everything within them, conservation areas must facilitate movement, migration, colonization and natural selection within our remaining natural systems in ways that isolate these systems from undue human influence.

Even in Canada, we aren't acting fast enough to what science is telling us. There is a real danger that our problems could get away on us simply because we didn't build a strong enough bridge between science and public policy. This is already happening in the U.S.

Dr. Henry Vaux chairs the Rosenberg International Forum on Water Policy and is the co-author of a recent National Academy of Sciences report on the future of water management in the United States. Dr. Vaux and his colleagues recently stated that "failure to do a better job of extending and communicating science and education could lead to a world overwhelmed by water problems even though the scientific information need to solve those problems might be in existence."

Imagine being overwhelmed by water management problems even though we have solutions to those problems in hand. Imagine being overwhelmed by biodiversity and climate issues even though we know what to do. We simply can't let that happen.

It has been estimated that it would cost $30-trillion a year to provide the planetary ecological services that nature presently provides to us for free. It might only cost 1/100 of that amount to protect and expand much of the world's existing ecological function. Viewed this way, E.O. Wilson argues, conserving biodiversity can be seen to be the best deal that nature has offered humanity since agriculture. It is time to play that card.

It has been noted in the widely publicized Stern Review on the Economics of Climate Change, that climate impacts could ultimately cost the global economy seven trillion dollars, more than the two World Wars and the Great Depression combined. Suddenly the ecological services provided free by the greater central Rockies ecosystem have a recognizable value. It is that value that we need to underscore.

Our future may be defined by our ability to manage our landscape and ecosystems in ways that delay, ameliorate and direct change toward ends we can live with. This means we need to know the path climate will take from present to future conditions, especially as they relate to water supply and quality. The best place to learn this is in the central Rockies ecosystem.

4. We need to build a strong local culture around ecosystem productivity

We can no longer afford to allow the public image of the greater central Rockies ecosystem to be defined solely by real estate developers, tourism promoters and recreational interests. While each of these has a role to play, they are not the only ones who should be defining sense of place in the mountain West for locals or the outside world. We have to use art, literature and popular culture, grounded in solid science, to inspire in the public imagination a new sense of pride in what we possess in terms of ecological wealth in the mountain West and why it is important to our future. We need to articulate a simple but sensible ecosystem ethic and communicate it outward in a way that will constantly reinforce local understanding of the value of what we possess in the mountain West that is unique to where and how we live.

We need high-profile public champions for the expanded bioregion. Every time we turn on a television or radio, we need to hear the message. I am not talking here about the worn-out *Hinterland Who's Who* that puts people to nostalgic sleep. We need some edge. We need to teach Westerners the value of what ecosystems do and provide — for us and for the world. And we need to do it now.

5. We have to redefine tourism and local culture around an understandable ecosystem ethic

It may be useful here to repeat the fact that within the Canadian Rockies World Heritage Site alone we have protected 27 mountain ranges, 669 prominent peaks, 12 major icefields and some 384 glaciers. Within this combined reserve are a total of 44 rivers, 164 named tributaries and 295 named lakes. Moreover, the region has been identified by the United Nations as being important to all of humanity by virtue of its importance to planetary ecosystem health.

If the tourism industry in and around the mountain national and provincial parks can't make a go of it with that kind of attraction at its core, then what do they need? To survive ecologically, which is also to say economically, we need to create a culture commensurate with the remarkable nature of the landscape we occupy. We can't do that without the sincere support of the tourism industry. The tourism industry, however, has to make this commitment without expecting every gesture in support of ecosystem understanding to be rewarded with further development approvals. Parks Canada executives cannot be rewarded solely on the basis of how much revenue their parks can earn. A larger ethic remains to be articulated in the mountain West while enough of its original character still exists. Having said that, it is important to observe that we may well be entering an era of neo-conservatism during which many of the most important values associated with national and provincial park protection may ultimately be under siege. We need only observe the United States to see what that looks like.

If we want to keep what we have, we will have to find ways to participate in the creation of an economic foundation compatible with an ecologically sound future. If we don't, then the future could take away from us all that we have worked for generations to protect. This suggests that we have to do a far better job of articulating the economic value of the ecological wealth we possess so that our whole society can redefine itself in the context of what that wealth might ultimately mean to them.

To that end it may also be timely to take the additional step of expanding the designation of the Canadian Rockies World Heritage Site.

6. Expand the Canadian Rockies World Heritage Site designation

In a recent study, Conservation International defined wilderness as an expanse of 10,000 square kilometres or more in which at least 70 per cent of the area still bears natural vegetation. We possess more than twice that much ecological wealth in the Canadian Rockies World Heritage Site alone. We will need more if we want to adapt to a changing climate.

During the consultation phase which resulted in the creation of the Canadian Rockies World Heritage Site, Alberta Provincial Parks indicated they would be supportive of adding 17 contiguous provincially protected areas to the designation. These areas, which include parks that buffer national parks along the Continental Divide all contain natural values similar and complementary to those found in the Canadian Rockies World Heritage Site.

The total area of these additions would be over 960,000 hectares, which would represent a more than 40 per cent increase in the total size of the site and would thus require a renomination. It was proposed in addition that three adjoining provincial parks in B.C. also be considered in any new nomination.

We are not talking about creating any new parks here, so no one has to be paranoid about anyone's objectives. What we are talking about is upgrading the status of what we already possess. We should do this in the name of watershed protection as well as in the name of improving our ability to create enough space for natural systems to evolve on their own in response to cumulative human effects and climate change. It may be this very act that presents the opportunity we need to demonstrate the value of the ecosystem services that such reserves generate, so that the economic value of our mountain national and provincial parks can be appropriately recognized.

Build extensive scientific research related to evolving ecosystem dynamics into the expansion of the designation. Link this research directly to further public education that underscores a vision of the West we want. Have public understanding of the economic value of properly functioning ecosystems inform evolving public policy and we will have created a foundation for this country's second great landscape-based national public policy achievement, a movement toward true sustainability.

It may sound impossible but we should remember what history tells us about the power of mountain places to define Western Canadian identity. We have done it once. We can do it again. But there is one last step.

7. Embody our society's need to be positive and persistent while being flexible and adaptive

Besides being concerned citizens, we all have community and family lives. Our knowledge of mountain geography and ecosystems allows us to be highly influential witnesses to climate impacts in our time and to extend that influence beyond the mountain community to everyone around us.

It will not just be our knowledge of mountains, however, that will influence others. Our trustworthiness as guides in the complex issue of our future will be determined by the extent to which we can all summon the qualities of character and personality that we so admire intergenerationally in those who have been granted grace by a lifelong exposure to mountain places and people.

Though it is important to be honest, it is also important to be considerate and positive in our outlook on our climate future. We must be flexible and adaptive to changing circumstances in the same way we would be while climbing a mountain.

Finally, we need to be persistent, as we will have to be in order to address the climate issue, if we want to achieve our goal. The longer we delay making necessary changes, the more gets invested in current systems and ideas and the more difficult making the needed changes becomes.

We have to dispel the myth that we can't do anything about what is happening, that we have to essentially sit back and watch as our world and everything that matters to us in it declines; that we have to accept diminishment and loss as the central theme of our historical era.

Now is not a time to be timid. We can't retreat, because there is no place to retreat to. Let's go up, not down. Let's expand our ecosystem ideal and see if, in making our ecological wealth apparent to ourselves and others, we can't shape a different kind of future than the one obviously approaching us. We've done it before. We can do it again. There is still room to move. We can still respond to what our water is telling us. It is still within our grasp to create the West we want.

Appendix *One*

25 Questions and Answers
Relating to Climate Change and Global Warming

as answered by
Dr. David Sauchyn
and
Bob Sandford
of the
Western Watersheds Climate Research Collaborative
May 28, 2007

1. **How can you say climate change is happening when our weather records only go back 50 years?**

     A number of scientific tools exist for plotting climate conditions backward in time far beyond weather records that exist at best only for the last century. We can analyze glacial advance and recession to tell us what climates were like in the past. We can also study lake and bog sediments, examine tree rings and analyze pollen. These tools also include ocean sediment records and records left in coral reefs, loess deposits and paleosols.

     If we want to go back even further we can analyze trapped air in ancient ice cores in Greenland or Antarctica. More sophisticated dating technologies such as radiocarbon and uranium series dating can also help us know what the climate was like in the distant past.

     All of these tools have been employed individually and together in the development of the climate models we have created to project climate change impacts in the future.

2. **I am a geologist and I know that climate has changed a lot over time and that this is nothing new.**

That the climate has changed in past geological epochs is a given. But it is important that this fact not lead us to inaction in the context of the warming trends we are seeing today. While humans have certainly survived significant climate change episodes in the past, never before have there been so many of us. Never before have all the habitable places have been so fully occupied. Never before have our material demands been so great. Never before in human history have our natural systems been so diminished and fragmented and so many species been threatened with extinction. The climate may have changed before, but there have never been so many of us and never have we been more vulnerable to its impacts.

3. **What is the difference between climate change and global warming?**

Climate change can be defined as any process, cyclical or otherwise, that causes the climate of the planet to warm or cool. When we are talking about global warming we are talking about trends toward higher mean annual temperatures. In talking about global warming in the context of the last century, we are talking about natural cyclical influences that are forcing warming, and about greenhouse gas emissions generated by humans that are accelerating this warming in our time.

4. **Isn't this just another environmentalist plot?**

To claim that the global threat is merely an environmentalist plot is absurd. While climate change may have at one time been an issue that existed primarily on the environmentalist agenda, it is no longer just an environmental concern. It is at once an environmental issue, an economic concern, a social disruption and a political challenge of a magnitude we have never faced before.

5. **If we survived climate change in the past, why is it such a big deal now?**

   As a society we are extremely vulnerable to climate change impacts. When faced with changes in climate in the past, humans moved uphill away from rising oceans or inland but always toward fresh water. Today, we can't just get up and move like we did in the past. In the places worth living in, someone already lives where we would seek to go. If circumstances develop as projected, there will be few places we can all move to and no wild nature we might return to.

   In this sense the global warming issue has produced a perfect storm of population pressure, economic expectation, ecosystem decline and jurisdictional atomization that could lead to serious consequences.

6. **How long has science known about global warming?**

   Remarkably, there is a strong historical link between mountaineering and the origins of climate science. The renowned Irish physicist John Tyndall was one of the most famous mountaineers of the 19th century.

   Tyndall's mountaineering interests extended to his scientific work when he began to focus on the "wondrous factory" that is the atmosphere. He was the first to discover the heat-absorbing qualities of both carbon dioxide and water vapour.

   In 1859, Tyndall also predicted that a water vapour feedback mechanism initiated by carbon dioxide could dramatically increase the mean temperature of the Earth's atmosphere. The carbon dioxide concentration in the atmosphere during Tyndall's time was only about 290 parts per million.

   It is now 2007. After nearly 150 years of extensive scientific research into all aspects of greenhouse gas impacts on climate, the Intergovernmental Panel on Climate Change reported acceleration of climate change effects.

   Carbon dioxide concentrations are now at about 380 parts per million, up about 30 per cent since John Tyndall first speculated on the importance of carbon dioxide to atmospheric temperature way back in 1859.

7. **How do we distinguish between natural climate change trends and human impacts?**

> The fact is that climate modellers can only reproduce current warming trends if they include the greenhouse gas emissions created by humans. If you exclude the effect of human beings on the atmosphere, then models show there should be no warming or even a slight cooling, when in fact mean temperatures are rising significantly.

8. **As CO_2 is a central compound in many life processes, how can it be considered a pollutant?**

> The history of our planetary life-support system is tied directly to the extent to which natural geological and biological processes are able to capture and store carbon dioxide. When atmospheric carbon dioxide concentrations remain within levels that can be accommodated by natural systems, carbon dioxide is not considered a pollutant. When humans generate carbon dioxide in concentrations that cannot readily be absorbed by oceans or by natural systems, these emissions can be classified as pollutants.

9. **What are greenhouse gases and what does each do?**

> The main greenhouse gases are carbon dioxide, methane, nitrous oxide, water vapour hydrofluorocarbons, perfluorocarbons and sulfur hexafluoride. They can be distinguished by their different capacities to trap heat and by the length of time they persist in the atmosphere. Carbon dioxide, though it does not capture heat as well as methane, is the most abundant of the greenhouse gases and stays in the atmosphere for as long as a century. Methane is 23 times more potent as a greenhouse gas than carbon dioxide but is less profuse and usually lasts only a month in the atmosphere. Nitrous oxides are also powerful greenhouse gases but are less prolific in the atmosphere and more localized in their impacts.

10. **How do CO_2 and other greenhouse gases cause lingering warming in the atmosphere?**

    Greenhouse gases trap radiation given off by the Earth and prevent it from escaping into space. A lot of this heat is stored in the oceans and is redistributed by ocean currents. It is this process that accounts for the lag in the effect greenhouse gases have on mean temperatures and why current greenhouse-gas-generated warming can be expected to last for centuries even if we were able to cut our emissions to zero immediately.

    If you have noticed that September and October temperatures in the Rockies are often summer-like even though the days are shorter and nights cooler, then you have observed part of the greenhouse effect on climate in this region.

11. **It appears that a lot of scientists and others still argue that climate change is not happening. Is there really consensus?**

    The Fourth Report of the Intergovernmental Panel on Climate Change, released in 2007, was the work of some 800 contributing authors, more than 400 lead authors from more than 130 countries, and more than 2,500 expert scientific reviewers. This IPCC work represents the longest and most vigorously peer-reviewed research project in the history of science.

    There is no longer any debate among practising climate science professionals that climate change is happening and that we humans are one of its principal causes.

12. **If climate change is really happening, why are some glaciers in Alaska continuing to grow?**

    At present, at least, there are some 160,000 glaciers in the world. It would be hard to imagine a situation somewhere in which proximity to a large body of water like an ocean did not, especially in the case of localized warming, result in enhanced winter precipitation that resulted in glacial advance. Because of this effect, some glaciers in the Yukon and Alaska are growing, as are glaciers in a few similar circumstances elsewhere. On the whole, however, glaciers are receding globally, especially at lower and mid-latitudes.

13. Why is there so much resistance from resource extraction and energy interests?

Professional public relations and lobbying are part of how business is done in our market economy. But there is a risk of being too good at it without keeping an eye on larger realities. We have all seen, for example, how effective lobbying ensured that North American automobile manufacturers remained exempt from legislation demanding more fuel-efficient vehicles. So successful has their lobby been that these companies have been permitted to keep producing inefficient cars and trucks even though it has hurt their business and our economy to do so. Because of persistent self-interest, North American auto manufacturers lost world domination of their own markets. We cannot let climate-related issues lead to similar misdirections and missed opportunities in other economic sectors in North America.

14. What about books like Michael Crichton's *State of Fear*? Shouldn't I believe them?

Not necessarily. The sensational nature of the global warming threat is simply too attractive for science-fiction writers, novelists and futurists to ignore. Authors of novelistic thrillers are entitled to use artistic licence in the creation of their plots and in their interpretation of science. While books like *State of Fear* hardly portray an accurate picture of contemporary climate science, they do bring the issue of global warming to the attention of a broader audience.

15. Isn't this a problem we should rely on technology to solve?

We have been spoiled on this continent by brilliant engineering and design. We really have. Good engineering and amazing technology solves our problems by proxy. You don't have to use less water, your tap will do it for you.

You don't have to drive less, your hybrid will reduce your
fuel consumption for you. But sooner or later technology
will not be enough. If we ultimately need to reduce our
energy consumption by 70 to 90 per cent, as some fore-
casts predict, global warming is going to demand that we
change some of our basic habits.

16. **Some experts are calling for a 70 to 90 per cent reduction
in energy consumption. How are we going to accomplish
that without destroying our economy?**

    A graph of the gross domestic product of the United
    States from 1900 to 2000 shows exponential growth in
    the economy. A graph of total water withdrawals in the
    United States over the same period shows that in the first
    part of the century — until about the late 1970s to early
    1980s — water use was in lockstep with economic growth.
    Population growth comes only with increased demand
    for water. But in the 1980s, the two curves split apart, and
    today the u.s. uses much less water per capita for every-
    thing than it used in the 1980s. A new idea has emerged:
    that you can break the link between economic develop-
    ment and increased water use.

    If you look at a similar graph of national energy use
    in the u.s. compared to per capita use in the state of
    California, you see the same trend. California has dem-
    onstrated that it can generate the same rate of economic
    growth while still dramatically reducing energy use and
    greenhouse gas emissions. If California can do this, then
    Alberta can do it. If the u.s. can do it, so can Canada. But
    we have to set out to try. We don't know what we are
    capable of until we are challenged.

17. **What simple things might we do to address the climate
change threat?**

    There are dozens of things an individual can do to reduce
    their personal energy consumption. Many can be accom-
    plished with no negative impact on our quality of life.
    Unfortunately, downloading all responsibility for climate
    change adaptation onto the individual citizen will not

result in the extent of reductions in greenhouse gases
we need to achieve to ensure reasonable climate stability.
As a society we need to think beyond energy efficiency
and renewable energy and move toward concepts of suf-
ficiency based on social and institutional reform and personal lifestyle changes that result in much less energy use
and much lower emissions of greenhouse gases. As individuals, we therefore need to press for effective public
policy that will create a framework of broader industry
and government participation in emissions reduction
that will make individual contributions meaningful.

18. Will carbon sequestration in abandoned oil and gas wells work?

Still in its infancy, large-scale geological sequestering of
carbon dioxide is being tested most rigorously in Norway.
Early indications are that, despite concerns over potential threats of leakage and water contamination, carbon
sequestration in abandoned oil and gas wells will work
in some circumstances. It is also possible that the use of
coal to generate electricity and the pumping of the captured carbon into wells to enhance production may work
to decrease CO_2 emissions while generating increased
oil production. However extensively employed, though,
these adaptations should be considered temporary measures only. Our real objective should be to develop abundant, emissions-free energy sources.

19. What about seeding the ocean with iron filings to absorb CO_2 in large amounts?

For billions of years oceans have been absorbing carbon
dioxide from the air. In what was later dubbed "the
Geritol solution," it was proposed that adding iron to sea
water — by spreading iron sulfate on the surface — would
result in greater capacity for carbon dioxide uptake. The
theory was that more iron would boost the appetite of
green algae for carbon dioxide, which would result in a
lower atmospheric concentration of CO_2. Unfortunately,
algae exposed to more iron in this way gave off as much

extra carbon dioxide as the marine plants had taken in. And that was without adding the impacts of having to transport all that iron sulfate all over the world and dumping it into our already ecologically troubled oceans.

20. Which companies are the big industrial contributors to CO_2 generation?

According to *Corporate Knights* magazine, the biggest industrial contributors of carbon dioxide emissions in Canada were in the sectors of electrical generation, and oil and gas production, transmission and distribution. In 2005, the magazine reported that the top ten emitters by company in Canada were:

1. Ontario Power Generation Inc.
2. Transalta Corp.
3. Canadian Utilities Ltd.
4. Saskatchewan Power Corp.
5. Imperial Oil Ltd.
6. Emera Inc.
7. TransCanada Corp.
8. EPCOR Power LP
9. Suncor Energy Inc.
10. New Brunswick Power Holding Corp.

. . .

18. Lafarge Canada Inc. [see the answer to Question 21 below as to cement plants]

21. How are carbon caps different from intensity targets?

Carbon caps are limits on the amount of carbon dioxide equivalents an industry or business is permitted to emit in a given time without penalty. Intensity targets are different. They are reductions not necessarily of actual total emissions but of the amount of carbon dioxide or its equivalents *per unit of production*. Large emitters such as cement plants favour intensity targets over carbon caps because these targets allow them to continue producing more cement as long as the amount of CO_2 they emit per tonne of cement produced decreases over time.

With appropriate incentives and careful monitoring and enforcement, intensity targets can gradually lead to reduced total emissions. Most often, however, such reductions are only achieved through emissions credits trading or mandatory ancillary activities that increase carbon sequestration in other ways.

The cement plant in the foothills of the Rockies at Exshaw, Alberta, for example, wants to expand its operations. Even though the net result will increase carbon dioxide emissions by 47 per cent or about half a million tonnes a year, the plant operators promise to achieve lower intensity targets, i.e., they will generate less carbon dioxide per tonne of product. Ideally, this wouldn't be permitted unless the operator makes up for the increase in emissions, and any earlier failures to reduce emissions, through other activities that compensate for the emissions produced in making cement.

22. What is the point of doing anything when the really big emitters like China and the u.s. aren't doing anything?

First of all, we stand to be accused of hypocrisy if we preach restraint to poorer countries without showing we are cutting our own emissions. If you ask the Chinese why they are not cutting emissions, their answer would be that they are struggling to generate the economic wealth that will one day allow them to afford to put in place the same kinds of environmental standards that presently exist in many parts of the developed world. They will point out that we too allowed deterioration of both air and water quality while we were developing the technology and wealth to be able to restore better conditions later.

It is a bit of a devil's bargain. The fear is that if historical patterns hold true, then in much of the developing world the more rapid economic growth stimulated by globalization will make pollution worse for quite some time before more growth begins to foster improvement.

The United States is a different story. As of 2007, their current federal government is opposed to any measures that will slow economic growth. This does not mean, however, that many Americans are not worried about the global warming threat. In the absence of federal leadership, cities and states across the U.S. are developing their own climate change adaptation and mitigation programs. This is also happening in Canada.

23. Kyoto has been a complete failure. Why worry about something we can't do anything about?

Our atmosphere is a global common-pool resource. The only way we can deal with global warming is through international cooperation. By 2004, 126 of the 136 countries that were parties to the crafting of the Kyoto Protocol had formally accepted the final agreement, including, as was required, countries accounting for 55 per cent of industrial countries' emissions of six designated gases. The treaty went into effect in February of 2005. In principle, the Kyoto Protocol required that 38 industrialized countries reduce their CO_2 emissions by at least 1.8 per cent by 2012.

While there were doubts expressed about whether the signatories would actually meet this target — and continuing debate about whether or not the Kyoto agreement constituted the right approach to the problem — the broader point remains that the great majority of nations around the world recognized that a problem exists and began a cooperative effort to address it. So in that sense Kyoto was not a failure.

Our failure has been that to date we have had neither the wisdom nor the foresight to replace the Kyoto Accord with something more effective.

24. I don't see any impacts where I live, so why should I worry?

If you live in the mountain West and you are not seeing climate change impacts, you are not looking. Spring is coming earlier each year, and winter snows, on average, are coming later. Glaciers are receding rapidly and conditions on high-altitude mountaineering routes are changing so quickly that climbing guides cannot keep up with the changes. The timing of rain and snowfall is changing, with more precipitation falling as rain in winter and longer dry periods with low river flows during late summer. Winter and nighttime temperatures are much milder.

Forest fires are occurring more frequently and with greater intensity. Treeline is rising and invasive species are becoming more abundant. Pest infestations such as the pine bark beetle are increasing in intensity and geographical distribution. Some mountain ecosystems have begun to disassemble and reassemble in unpredictable ways. Species such as the mountain caribou are threatened with extinction.

Climate-related changes in the ecosystems of the Rocky Mountains are profound, and many people who know and love these mountains are deeply concerned.

25. The big impacts are not expected until later in the century. I'll be dead by then. Why should I worry?

Don't count on missing the show. Climate impacts are accelerating at rates that far exceed almost all initial projections. We won't have to wait for the next generation for the opening act. Why should we worry? We should worry because our children and their children are going to inherent the consequences of our actions. To fail to respect our obligation to future generations would be a morally unacceptable act.

The Big Question: What Can I Do?

This is an issue in which the individual can make a real difference to the outcome. If you are concerned about climate change, do what you can to reduce the amount of energy and water you use. By exemplifying appropriate habits and attitudes, you can influence the direction our society will take with respect to what is happening, what it means and how we should react to the climate change and global warming problem What an individual does matters.

Appendix *Two*

What You Can Do to Save Water

1. **Individuals *can* do something about conserving and using water wisely!**

   Surrounded by seemingly unlimited freshwater resources, Canadians are the world's most wasteful water users. In reality, our supplies of clean, usable water are limited, and we must learn to use them more wisely if we are to continue to enjoy the benefits they provide. Water conservation begins at home, and you can do your share by observing the following DOS and DON'TS in and around the house.

   What better place to start to use water wisely than in our own homes? It's where we spend most of our time and where we have the most control over how things are done.

   In the kitchen:
   - Use an aerator and/or a flow-reducer attachment on your tap to reduce your water usage.
   - Always turn taps off tightly so they do not drip.
   - Promptly repair any leaks in and around your taps. (One leak can waste several thousand litres of water per year.)
   - When hand-washing dishes, never run water continuously. Wash dishes in a partially filled sink and then rinse them using the spray attachment on your tap.
   - If you have an electric dishwasher, use it only to wash full loads, and use the shortest cycle possible. Many dishwashers have a conserver/water-miser cycle.
   - When cleaning fruit and vegetables, never do so under a continuously running tap. Wash them in a partially filled sink and then rinse them quickly under the tap.
   - When boiling vegetables, save water by using just enough to cover them and using a tightly fitting lid.

- Keep a bottle of drinking-water in your fridge instead of running your tap until the water gets cool each time you want some water. Do not forget to rinse the container and renew the water every two to three days.

In the bathroom:

About 65 per cent of indoor home water use occurs in our bathrooms, and toilets are the single greatest water users.

- When washing or shaving, partially fill the sink and use that water rather than running the tap continuously. (This saves about 60 per cent of the water normally used.) Use short bursts of water to clean razors.

- When brushing your teeth, turn the water off while you are actually brushing instead of running it continuously. Then use the tap again for rinsing and use short bursts of water for cleaning your brush. (This saves about 80 per cent of the water normally used.)

- Always turn taps off tightly so they do not drip.

- Promptly repair any leaks in and around taps.

- Use aerators and/or flow-reducer devices on all your taps.

- Use either low-flow shower heads or adjustable flow-reducers on your shower heads. (They diminish flow by at least 25 per cent.)

- Take short showers — turn off the water while you are soaping and shampooing and then rinse off quickly. Some shower heads have a shut-off lever that allows you to maintain the water pressure and temperature when you stop the flow.

- Short showers use less water than baths, but if you still prefer bathing, avoid overfilling the tub.

- Reduce water usage by about 20 per cent by placing a weighted plastic bottle filled with water in the water tank of your toilet. Low-cost "inserts" for the toilet tank are an alternative to plastic bottles. With a toilet insert, a family of four could save 45,000 litres of water per year. Toilet inserts are available at most hardware and plumbing supply stores.

- You can reduce water usage by 40 to 50 per cent by installing low-flush toilets.

- Flush your toilet only when really necessary. Never use the toilet as a garbage can to dispose of cigarette butts, paper tissues etc.

- Check regularly for toilet tank leaks into the toilet bowl by putting a small amount of food colouring into the tank and observing whether it spreads into the bowl without flushing. Repair leaks promptly. Ensure that the float ball is properly adjusted so that the tank water level does not exceed the height of the overflow tube. Also, periodically examine whether the plunge ball and flapper valve in the tank are properly seated, and replace parts when necessary.

- Regularly check for leaks at the base of your toilet and have any promptly repaired.

- Never flush garbage of any kind down the toilet. Household cleaners, paints, solvents, pesticides and other chemicals can be very harmful to the environment, and paper diapers, dental floss, plastic tampon holders etc. can create problems at sewage treatment plants.

- Locate your water meter and periodically record the reading late in the evening and again early the next morning between any water use. Then compare the readings to see whether there was any water leakage during the night. If so, track it down and have it repaired.

In the laundry room:

- Wash only full loads in your washing machine.

- Use the shortest cycle possible for washing clothes, and use the "suds saver" feature if your machine has one.

- If your washer has an adjustable water-level indicator, set the dial to use only as much water as is really necessary.

- If you have a septic system, spread out your washing to avoid heavy-use days that could overload the system.

- Use only cleaning products that will not harm the environment when they are rinsed away after use. Look for "environmentally friendly" products when shopping.

- Promptly repair any leaks around the taps, hoses or fittings of your washer or the taps of your laundry sink.

In the yard and garden:

- Lawns and gardens require only 5 mm of water per day during warm weather. Less is needed during spring, fall and cool weather.

- Water lawns every three to five days rather than for a short period every day. In warm weather, apply 5 mm of water for each day since the last watering.

- The amount of water applied can be easily measured by placing a can in the area being sprinkled. Measure the time required to apply the proper amount of water and use this information for future sprinkling.

- Grass that is green does not need water. Water is required when the grass starts to develop a black tinge along the top. Recovery is almost immediate when water is applied at this stage. Blackening does not hurt grass; browning does.

- Do not overwater in anticipation of a shortage. Soil cannot store extra water.

- Use shut-off timers or on/off timers if possible. Do not turn on sprinklers and depart for the day.

- Water during the cool part of the day, in the morning or evening. Do not water on windy days.

- Keep your lawns healthy and maintain them at a height of 6.5 cm. Taller grass holds water better, and a healthy lawn will choke out weeds.

- Young or freshly transplanted garden plants need small quantities of water more frequently until they are well established.

- Most shrubs and young trees need water only once per week, even in warm weather.

- Wash your vehicle only when absolutely necessary.

- Clean sidewalks and driveways with a broom, not a hose.

In the bush:

- Do not wash in the lake or river.

- Wash your dishes away from the water's edge, moving into the bush approximately 10 m. Use sand instead of soap to scrub them clean.

- Do not dump waste food or garbage into the water.
- Clean fish well away from the water's edge.
- Build latrines well back from the water's edge.
- If a latrine is needed only for temporary use, dig a shallow pit approximately 15 cm deep at least 10 m away from the water's edge and cover it with earth before moving on.
- Dig shallow pits approximately 15 cm deep, to bury compostable waste such as food waste or fish guts. Or burn waste to avoid attracting animals.
- Pack out all non-degradable waste such as cans, bottles, tinfoil and plastic.
- Fill outboard motors over land, not over water.
- Consider using an electric motor or a canoe instead of a gasoline motor.

For more information on ways you can use water more efficiently in your home, consult the Environment Canada publication *Water: No Time to Waste — A Consumer's Guide to Water Conservation,* available in print from:

> Enquiry Centre
> Environment Canada
> Ottawa, Ontario K1A 0H3
> Tel.: (819) 997-2800
> Toll free: 1-800-668-6767
> Fax: (819) 953-2225
> E-mail: enviroinfo@ec.gc.ca
>
> and on the Internet from
> www.ec.gc.ca/water/en/info/pubs/nttw/e_nttwi.htm

2.   Avoid using hazardous household products

Most proprietary household chemicals are safe and environmentally friendly when used according to the directions on the package. However, some have a harmful cumulative effect on the environment when they are overused or incorrectly disposed of.

- Buy only those environmentally hazardous products you really need, and buy them in quantities you will be able to completely use up so you will not have to worry about disposing of leftovers later.

- Additional information on non-hazardous household products and their uses can be obtained from the following and similar organizations:

Canadian Manufacturers of Chemical Specialties Association
56 Sparks Street, Suite 500
Ottawa, Ontario K1P 5A9
Tel.: (613) 232-6616
Fax: (613) 233-6350
E-mail: morinm@cmcs.org

Consumers Association of Canada
267 O'Connor Street, Suite 307
Ottawa, Ontario K2P 1V3
Tel.: (613) 238-2533
Fax: (613) 563-2254
E-mail: info@consumer.ca
www.consumer.ca

The federal government endorses products that are environmentally responsible. Look for the Environmental Choice EcoLogo™. Products bearing this label have been tested and certified by the Environmental Choice Program. Each dove represents a sector of society — consumers, industry and government — linked together to improve and protect the environment. The logo identifies the products that maximize energy efficiency and the use of recycled or recyclable materials and minimize the use of environmentally hazardous substances. Consumers can make informed choices. For more information, contact:

Environmental Choice Program
Terra-Choice Environmental Services Inc.
1280 Old Innes Road, Suite 801
Ottawa, Ontario K1B 5M7
Tel.: (613) 247-1900
Toll free: 1-800-478-0399
Fax: (613) 247-2228
E-mail: ecoinfo@terrachoice.ca
www.environmentalchoice.com/

3. Don't misuse your household's sewage system

If you do not want toxic chemicals in household products harming the environment and even coming back to you in your water or your food, dispose of them properly.

- Always try to use completely, or recycle to other people, all of the contents of such products as oven cleaners, toilet bowl cleaners, sink drain cleaners, bleaches, rust removers and most other acidic and alkaline products. This also includes paints, solvents, carpet and furniture cleaners, polishes and glues.

- Such items as disposable diapers, dental floss, plastic tampon holders and hair can create many problems in the sewage treatment plant; they should all be tossed into the wastebasket, not the toilet.

- Your local fire department will normally accept unwanted leftovers of barbecue starter fluids, lighter fluids, gasoline and furnace oils.

- Where possible, choose latex (water-based) paint instead of oil-based paint. Use it up instead of storing or dumping it.

4. Avoid the use of pesticides and hazardous materials in your garden and yard

Some pesticides and hazardous materials accumulate in the groundwater and food chain and are toxic to various forms of life, particularly when they are not used according to the directions specified on the package or when the empty containers are disposed of without proper precautions.

- Reduce or avoid the use of pesticides to control household or garden pests by employing more environmentally responsible methods such as

  ~ pulling weeds by hand;
  ~ pulling off and disposing of infested leaves;
  ~ picking off larvae;
  ~ using an insecticidal soap solution to dislodge or suffocate insects, or dislodging them with a stream of water from a garden hose;

~ rotating garden crops each year to prevent depletion of soil nutrients and control soil-borne diseases;

~ cultivating your garden. Regular hoeing will control weeds and keep plants healthy and more resistant to insects.

- Use natural fertilizers such as bonemeal or compost.
- Spread sand rather than salt on your sidewalks and driveways to get traction on winter ice.

5. Don't dump hazardous products into storm drains

Storm drains empty into underground storm sewer systems, discharging directly into nearby lakes and streams, which are important habitat for fish and wildlife. Unlike domestic wastes collected by sanitary sewers, the contents of storm sewers are generally not treated at sewage treatment plants prior to their discharge into a stream or lake. Therefore, dispose of oils, detergents, paints, solvents and other products at local recycling or disposal facilities. Some communities organize special days for collecting these wastes or have their own hazardous-waste collection sites. Contact your health and environment officers or local waste disposal company for times and places. If your community doesn't have either, promote the idea.

6. Don't sit back and just let things happen

An informed and committed public can become a powerful constituency in support of environmentally concerned political leaders, and even by themselves can provide a catalyst for environmental issues. You can make a difference!

- Become informed.
- Trust in the ability of the individual to take action on environmental issues, and work together with other individuals, experts and politicians.
- Be willing to change your attitudes, behaviours and expectations.

- Join and support local and national groups that work to solve environmental problems on institutional, national and international levels. There are about 1,800 such groups across Canada.

- Urge and support federal, provincial and municipal action on environmental issues.

- Do not use products that are harmful to the environment. Urge stores to abandon wasteful packaging and use biodegradable materials.

- Exercise your rights as a citizen: request information, participate in public hearings, serve on advisory committees and address review boards. Under federal legislation, these options are available under the terms of the Canada Water Act, the Canadian Environmental Protection Act, 1999, and the national Flood Damage Reduction Program. There are others . . .

- When voting in municipal, provincial and federal elections, make your choices based on the environmental views, positions and practices of the candidates.

- Educate your children and your friends. Environmental problems cannot be solved in a single generation; your children and their children will have to carry on the work.

We welcome readers' comments about the Primer. These can be sent to the address below. To obtain copies of the Primer and/or a list of other publications on water, please contact:

Enquiry Centre
Environment Canada
Ottawa, Ontario K1A 0H3
Tel.: (819) 997-2800
Toll free: 1-800-668-6767
Fax: (819) 953-2225
E-mail: enviroinfo@ec.gc.ca
www.ec.gc.ca/water/en/info/pubs/e_pubs.htm

Written on the Wind:
A Climate-Change Bookshelf

Film/video
An Inconvenient Truth: A Global Warning. Dir. Davis Guggenheim. Prod. Participant Productions and Lawrence Bender Productions. Paramount, 2006.

What's Up with the Weather? Dir. Jon Palfreman. Prod. Frontline/Nova Productions. WGBH/Public Broadcasting Service (U.S.), 2000.

Books
Alley, Richard B. *The Two-Mile Time Machine: Ice Cores, Abrupt Change & Our Future.* Princeton, N.J.: Princeton University Press, 2000.

Linden, Eugene. *The Winds of Change: Climate, Weather and the Destruction of Civilizations.* New York: Simon & Schuster, 2006.

Ruddiman, William F. *Earth's Climate Past and Future.* New York: W.H. Freeman, 2001.

Ruddiman William F. *Plows, Plagues & Petroleum: How Humans Took Control of Climate.* Princeton, N.J.: Princeton University Press, 2005.

Rutter, Nat, Murray Coppold and Dean Rokosh. *Climate Change and Landscape in the Canadian Rocky Mountains.* Field, B.C.: The Burgess Shale Geoscience Foundation, 2006.

Sherman, Joe. *Gasp! The Swift and Terrible Beauty of Air.* Washington, D.C.: Shoemaker & Hoard, 2004.

Weart, Spencer R. *The Discovery of Global Warming.* Cambridge, Mass.: Harvard University Press, 2003.

Landmarks in the ongoing discussion
Gelbspan, Ross. *Boiling Point: How Politicians, Big Oil and Coal, Journalists and Activists Have Fueled the Climate Crisis, and What We Can Do To Avoid Disaster.* New York: Basic Books, 2004.

McIntosh, Roderick J., Joseph Tainter and Susan Keech McIntosh, eds. *The Way The Wind Blows: Climate, History & Human Action.* New York: Columbia University Press, 2000.

Speth, James Gustave. *Red Sky at Morning: America and the Crisis of the Global Environment.* New Haven, Conn.: Yale University Press, 2004.

The evidence becomes clearer and clearer
Bowen, Mark. *Thin Ice: Unlocking the Secrets of Climate in the World's Highest Mountains.* New York: Henry Holt & Co., 2005.

Flannery, Tim. *The Weather Makers: How We Are Changing the Climate and What It Means for Life on Earth.* New York: HarperCollins, 2005.

Kolbert, Elizabeth. *Field Notes from a Catastrophe*. London: Bloomsbury Books, 2006.

Lovelock, James. *The Revenge of Gaia: Why the Earth Is Fighting Back – And How We Can Still Save Humanity*. London: Allen Lane/Penguin Books, 2006.

Monbiot, George. *Heat: How to Stop the Planet from Burning*. Scarborough, Ont.: Doubleday Canada, 2006.

Motavalli, Jim, ed. *Feeling the Heat: Dispatches from the Frontlines of Climate Change*. Oxford: Routledge, 2004.

Pearce, Fred. *The Last Generation: How Nature Will Take Its Revenge for Climate Change*. Toronto: Key Porter Books, 2007.

Romm, Joseph. *Hell and High Water: Global Warming – The Solution and the Politics and What We Should Do*. New York: William Morrow, 2007.

Climate change from a European perspective

Lynas, Mark. *High Tide: The Truth about Our Climate Crisis*. New York: Picador, 2004.

McDonagh, Seán. *Climate Change: The Challenge of All of Us*. Dublin: The Columba Press, 2006.

The economics of climate change

Friedman, Benjamin M. *The Moral Consequences of Economic Growth*. New York: Vintage Books, 2006.

Stern, Nicholas. *The Economics of Climate Change: The Stern Review*. Cambridge, U.K., and New York: Cambridge University Press, 2007.

Climate change and public policy

Dessler, Andrew E., and Edward A. Parson. *The Science and Politics of Global Climate Change: A Guide to the Debate*. Cambridge, U.K., and New York: Cambridge University Press, 2006.

A fine picture book

Ochoa, George, Jennifer Hoffman and Tina Tin. *Climate: The Force that Shapes Our World and the Future of Life on Earth*. London: Rodale International, 2005.

Dark departures: fiction

Crichton, Michael. *State of Fear*. New York: HarperCollins, 2004.

Lynch, Jim. *The Highest Tide*. London: Bloomsbury Books, 2005.

Tushingham, Mark. *Hotter Than Hell*. Saint John, N.B.: Dreamcatcher Publishing, 2005.

Dark departures: non-fiction

Benton, Michael J. *When Life Nearly Died: The Greatest Mass Extinction of All Time*. London: Thames & Hudson, 2003.

Diamond, Jared. *Collapse: How Societies Choose To Fail or Succeed*. New York: Viking, 2005.

Homer-Dixon, Thomas. *Environment, Scarcity and Violence*. Princeton, N.J.: Princeton University Press, 1999.

Kunstler, James Howard. *The Long Emergency: Surviving the Converging Catastrophes of the Twenty-First Century*. New York: Atlantic Monthly Press, 2005.

Martin, James. *The Meaning of the 21st Century: A Vital Blueprint for Ensuring Our Future*. Bodelva, Cornwall, U.K.: Eden Project Books, 2006.

Tainter, Joseph A. *The Collapse of Complex Societies*. Cambridge, U.K.: Cambridge University Press, 1988.

Optimistic visions
Homer-Dixon, Thomas. *The Upside of Down: Catastrophe, Creativity and the Renewal of Civilization*. Toronto: Alfred A. Knopf Canada, 2006.

Books of dubious value
Joseph, Lawrence E. *Apocalypse 2012: A Scientific Investigation into Civilization's End*. New York: Morgan Road Books, 2007.

Kotter, John, and Holger Rathgeber, with artwork by Peter Mueller. *Our Iceberg Is Melting: Changing and Succeeding under Any Conditions*. New York: St. Martin's Press, 2005.

Good works on important climate-related topics
Emanuel, Kerry. *Divine Wind: The History and Science of Hurricanes*. New York: Oxford University Press, 2005.

Giroux, Henry A. *Stormy Weather: Katrina and the Politics of Disposability*. Boulder, Colo.: Paradigm Publishers, 2006.

McGuffie, Kendal, and Ann Henderson-Sellers, *Climate Modelling: A Climate Modelling Primer*. Chichester, West Sussex, U.K.: John Wiley & Sons, 2005. (includes CD-ROM)

Reed, Betsy, ed. *Unnatural Disaster:* The Nation *on Hurricane Katrina*. New York: Nation Books, 2006.

Safina, Carl. *Song for the Blue Ocean*. New York: Henry Holt & Co., 1997.

Sustainable energy
Jaccard, Mark. *Sustainable Fossil Fuels: The Unusual Suspect in the Quest for Clean and Enduring Energy*. Cambridge, U.K., and New York: Cambridge University Press, 2005.

IPCC Reports
United Nations Intergovernmental Panel on Climate Change. All reports are available for download from www.ipcc.ch. Geneva: IPCC Secretariat, c/o World Meteorological Organization.

Index

Acknowledgments

This book would not have been written without the support of a great many people. The success of the United Nations Water for Life initiative in Canada has been predicated principally on the support of two organizations: the University of Lethbridge and the Canadian Water Network. I am particularly indebted to Dr. Dennis Fitzpatrick, Vice-President of Research at the University of Lethbridge, who allowed our program to become imbedded in the university's outstanding water research program and larger public policy initiatives. I am also indebted to Mark Servos and David Cotter at the Canadian Water Network, who gave national support and profile to this initiative. The passion these people express for the translation of scientific research into language the public can understand and act upon allowed me to meet and work with a broad range of equally knowledgeable and committed people in the field of water all over Canada.

It is impossible to understand how water is used in this country without understanding the needs of the agriculture industry. To that end I am utterly indebted to David Hill of the Alberta Irrigation Projects Association, who took it upon himself to educate me as much and as quickly as possible about agricultural practices relating to water use in Canada and about the politics of water management in Western Canada. Through Mr. Hill I was introduced to other experts, such as Jim Webber and Jim Czabay, who were equally accommodating in sharing their understanding about how water is managed and how it will be managed in the future.

I also owe a debt of gratitude to Lorne Fitch, the founder of the Cows and Fish riparian habitat restoration program, and to Dan Sheer of Hydrologics Inc., who early in the development of the UN Water for Life initiative demonstrated to me how important patience was to success in exploring how changes of habit and policy are made to happen in a complex society.

Through this initiative I have learned how important it will be to ensure that decisions we make about our future are based first on scientific knowledge about what is happening to our water and weather. This book owes a great debt to a number of prominent scientists. I would especially like to thank the tireless Hans Schreier and the energetic Sandra Brown at the University of British Columbia, whose commitment to knowledge and action on water issues is without boundaries.

For their commitment, knowledge and willingness to share perspectives and experience I am much indebted to David Sauchyn and

Norman Henderson of the Prairie Adaptation Research Collaborative at the University of Regina. I owe a debt of thanks also to Jim Byrne, Joe Rasmussen, Alice Hontella, Hester Jiskoot, Stewart Rood and Dan Johnson at the University of Lethbridge, the "research home" for the United Nations Water for Life initiative in Canada.

For their willingness to share information on water in relation to climate change I am indebted especially to the members of the Western Watershed Climate Research Collaborative science advisory committee, who include David Sauchyn of the University of Regina, Dr. David Schindler of the University of Alberta, Dr. Shawn Marshall of the University of Calgary, Dr. Jim Byrne of the University of Lethbridge, Dr. David Rodenhuis of the Pacific Climate Impacts Consortium and Dr. Henry Baltes of the Swiss Federal Institute of Technology in Zurich.

For mentoring me on matters relating to public policy and water in North America and around the world I will never be able to repay the debt I owe to Henry Vaux, a retired Vice-President of the University of California system who is presently the Chair of the Rosenberg International Forum on Water Policy. Related to the Rosenberg Forum, I would also like to thank Helen Ingram of the University of Arizona in Tucson, who unselfishly shared a lifetime of experience and wise insight into water policy issues. For sharing his profound knowledge about how to translate science into effective public policy, I also owe a great debt to David Eaton of the Lyndon Johnson School of Public Policy at the University of Texas in Austin.

I must also acknowledge key partners in the United Nations Water for Life Decade in Canada. I have been taught a great deal about public perception of water issues by Craig Ikeda of Global Television, and by Director of Photography Peter Ladiges, who worked closely with our initiative for five years to produce two series of regional and national television campaigns aimed at dispelling the myth of limitless water abundance in Canada. I would also like to thank Kelly Hartmann and Alyssa Chomick of Hartmann Design, who went to extraordinary lengths to create a website that would give meaning and value to the television campaigns. To see the television campaign and to link to information about water in Canada, visit the UN Water for Life Decade website at www.thinkwater.ca.

I would also like to offer very special thanks to Denise Carpenter and Stephen Stanley of EPCOR, who lent support to the UN Water for Life initiative and extended to me every opportunity to learn as much as I could about water quality, treatment and supply.

I also owe a debt of thanks to Kindy Gosal, Josh Smienk and Garry Merkel of the Columbia Basin Trust for their unflagging support for the UN Water for Life initiative and for sharing their science and knowledge about the history and nature of their remarkable basin. In this context I would also like to thank Alan Hamlet at the Climate Impacts Group at the University of Washington in Seattle for his insights into climate impacts on water resources in the mountain regions of the West.

I would also like to offer special thanks to Karen Kun of Waterlution in Toronto, and to *Corporate Knights* magazine, who together have done a great deal to promote and advance the work of the UN Water for Life initiative. Special thanks are also owed to Brenda Lucas and the Walter and Gordon Duncan Foundation.

For their sharing of information and perspective and for the sheer commitment they make to water management I would like to thank the British Columbia Ministry of the Environment, Alberta Environment, and the Manitoba Ministry of Water Stewardship. I would also like to thank Niagara Flapperless Water Conservation Solutions and City of Toronto Water for their contribution to our knowledge base and their support for the UN Water for Life Decade. In addition, I would like to express my thanks to Dave Verhulst and Ronna Schneberger of the Mountain Parks Heritage Interpretation Association for supporting early research into climate change impacts in the mountain national parks.

I would be remiss if I did not thank Don Gorman at Rocky Mountain Books for believing so wholeheartedly in this book, and Joe Wilderson, also of RMB, who not only offered valuable editorial advice but also took a lively and witty interest in many of the issues this book explores.

Finally, I must especially thank my wife, Vi, and my children, Reid, Amery and Landon, for their sacrifices during long periods of uncertainty associated with the conception of the United Nations Water for Life initiative in Canada, the subsequent birth of the Western Watersheds Climate Research Collaborative and the writing of the book. Without the unconditional support of my family this book would not have been written.

While all of the above, and too many others to name, offered information and support that was ultimately expressed in the form of this book, none is responsible for any errors or omissions that may exist here. For these and for all interpretations of current scientific knowledge stated herein, the author alone must take responsibility.

**The author wishes to express gratitude
to the following organizations:**

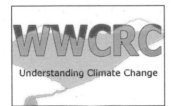

≈

Bob Sandford is the author or editor of some 20 books on the history and heritage of the Canadian West. He began his work with UN-linked initiatives as chair of the United Nations International Year of Mountains in 2002. He also chaired the United Nations International Year of Fresh Water and Wonder of Water Initiative in Canada in 2003/04. These celebrations focused on the growing importance of water to ecological and cultural heritage in Canada.

Bob is presently chair of the United Nations International Decade "Water for Life" Partnership in Canada, an initiative that aims to advance long-term water quality and availability issues in response to climate change in this country and abroad. He is also director of the Western Watersheds Climate Research Collaborative, a research and public-policy arm of the University of Lethbridge that promotes understanding of climate impacts on river systems originating in the Rocky Mountains. Bob was the first Canadian to be invited to sit on the advisory committee for the Rosenberg International Forum on Water Policy, a biennial global public-policy forum that examines solutions to our planet's water crisis.

≈